25.⁰⁰

P9-BZB-462

THE LEGENDARY ARTISTS OF TAOS

THE LEGENDARY ARTISTS OF TAOS

Expanded from the Pages of American Artist
By Mary Carroll Nelson

WATSON-GUPTILL PUBLICATIONS/NEW YORK

First published 1980 in the United States and Canada by Watson-Guptill Publications,
a division of Billboard Publications, Inc.,
1515 Broadway, New York, N.Y. 10036

Library of Congress Cataloging in Publication Data
Nelson Mary Carroll.
  The legendary artists of Taos.
  Bibliography: p.
  Includes index.
  I. Taos school of art. 2. Artists—New Mexico—
Biography. 3. Art, Modern—20th century—New
Mexico. I. American artist. II. Title.
N6512.T34N44   759.18953 [B]   80-15887
ISBN 0-8230-2745-7

Manufactured in Japan

First Printing, 1980

For Ed

Acknowledgments

I would like to thank the following people for their courteous and generous contributions to this book:

Louise M. Abrums	Laura Gilpin	Irene Rawlings
Eugene B. Adkins	Calista Hillman	Doel Reed
Paul Benisek	Stephen L. Good	Edna Robertson
Helen Greene Blumenschein	Ellen Greene	Fred A. Rosenstock
Mary Blumenthal	Mrs. E. Martin Hennings	Edward Sackett
Jack K. Boyer	Lawrence O. Hogrefe	Mr. and Mrs. Toy Dixon Savage, Jr.
Janet Burdick	Donald Humphrey	Patricia Sayles
Bill Beutler	Gene Kloss	Irma and Richard Schuler
Dr. Everett Campbell	Barbara Latham	Bonnie Silverstein
James V. and Mary L. Carroll	James Levy	Dorothy Spencer
Howard Cook	Ila McAfee	Israel Stein
Regina Tatum Cooke	Susan E. Meyer	Mrs. Edgar Tobin
Alfred Dasburg	Jonathan A. Meyers	Robert L.B. Tobin
Ivan Dunton	Constance Modrall	Louise B. Young
Patricia Deaton	Suzanne Nelson	Robert R. White
Kit and Ted Egri	Wendell Ott	John B. Wilkinson
Harrison Eiteljorg	Dr. William P. O'Grady	Carole D. Wilson
Forrest Fenn	Gerald P. Peters	Mr. and Mrs. Woodrow Wilson
Bob Fillie	Marlou Quintana	

and a special thanks to Donald Holden and Marsha Melnick who have supported the concept for the book as Editorial Directors of Watson-Guptill Publications.

Contents

THE TAOS ART COLONY

TAOS VALLEY is a wide, flat plain in northern New Mexico, 7000 feet above sea level. To the northeast are the pine-covered Sangre de Cristo mountains, looming sharply in a series of probing triangles. To the west, the Rio Grande cuts ever deeper in its narrow gorge as it tumbles its way south.

Two impressions make their impact on first viewing this scene: the pastel tints of the sky, mesa land, and mountains bleached by the intensely bright sunlight are unexpectedly delicate, and the vista is tremendous. The view is made dramatic and changeable by swiftly moving clouds that throw sharp shadow patterns across the desert.

Both the Spanish village of Taos and the Taos Indian pueblo are built close to the mountains. Using identical materials, the Indians and the Spanish each created an indigenous architecture well-suited to the locale.

Hundreds of years before the Spanish Conquistadors discovered New Mexico, the Taos pueblo was already standing. Its adobe rooms rise one upon the other in clifflike form. Beams protrude from the walls, their shadows slanting across the adobe. Ladders and chimneys add detail to these ancient apartment houses. Gray smoke curls from the chimneys and from outdoor ovens that are dotted about like beehives in front of the buildings. Every so often a shawl-clad woman or blanket-wrapped man walks with dignity across the packed earth between the pueblo and the creek. This description is accurate today, and it was also true at the end of the 19th century.

Indians and Spanish settlers of Taos aided one another and shared their knowledge. Indian farmers raised corn, chili, beans, and squash. Spanish farmers brought livestock with them and seeds to plant wheat. Straw from the wheat made their bricks stronger than those of the Indians. There was an exchange. Aspects of the Spanish culture—clothing, outdoor *hornos* (the ovens used at the pueblo), livestock, and Catholicism—made changes in the Indian lifestyle. On the other hand, food introduced to them by the Indians became the diet of the Spanish. Farming was the main occupation of both people. Despite the antipathies that may have existed between them, they also had an on-going, well-established rapport.

Into this community in 1898 came Ernest L. Blumenschein and Bert Phillips, the men who began the legend of the Taos art colony. When they arrived, only about 25 Anglos resided in the village. Thirty years later the little town was known worldwide as a magnetic center where many artists lived or visited. Each artist who came followed a legend of growth and change that led inexorably to Taos, and each remains identified with the village.

In 1912, the year New Mexico became a state, six men founded the influential professional club called the Taos Society of Artists. They were: Joseph Henry Sharp, Bert Phillips, Ernest L. Blumenschein, Oscar E. Berninghaus, E. Irving Couse, and W. Herbert Dunton.

In later years they invited Victor Higgins, Walter Ufer, Catherine Carter Critcher, E. Martin Hennings, and Kenneth M. Adams to become members. The group thrived until March 1927, when the membership present decided the society was no longer needed.

According to their charter, the purpose of the TSA was "to develop a high standard of art among its members, and to aid in the diffusion of taste for art in general...[and] to facilitate bringing before the public through exhibitions and other means, tangible results of the work of its members." To be accepted, the artist had to win a prize in a major exhibition, and the other members had to know and approve of the artist's work and reputation.

In 1914 the TSA organized the first exhibition in the Palace of the Governors at Santa Fe. Afterward they sent their work around the country on circuit shows, where it caught on immediately. Participating galleries, groups, organizations, and museums agreed to cover all shipping costs; they received a commission of 20 percent on sales. Works sold at the shows were replaced with more paintings by the artists.

To get the canvases out of Taos was no easy job. They were sent overland in the wagon owned by John Dunn, an early character of Taos who maintained the one dependable link with the outside world. The wagon delivered the crates to the nearest railhead at Tres Piedras. In those days a trip from Taos to Santa Fe, along a rough track in the Rio Grande gorge, took two days; yet twice each year the TSA sent their shows eastward, sometimes abroad, and members of the group entered the major shows in New York and Chicago, where they won top awards and monetary prizes.

Visitor (center) at the Taos Pueblo, early 1900s. The Lucinda Martin Iliff Collection, Kit Carson Memorial Foundation, Taos.

Talpa, New Mexico, just south of Taos in Taos Valley.

Looking south at the Taos Pueblo. Fenn Galleries Ltd., Santa Fe.

On-lookers at the Taos Pueblo. Fenn Galleries Ltd., Santa Fe.

San Geronimo Day, Taos Pueblo, early 1900s. The Lucinda Martin Iliff Collection, Kit Carson Memorial Foundation, Taos.

KENNETH M. ADAMS, the last member to join the TSA before it was dissolved, wrote in the *New Mexico Quarterly*: "The fame of the Society was not a slow and painful growth. Recognition and favorable publicity came to the Taos group immediately after its organization."

Adams analyzed the impact of the Taos painters as follows: "Art at this time had not crossed the Mississippi westward. Men creating it lived in eastern states because they felt the need of close association with both dealers and museums .... Consequently, a group of painters living in a little New Mexico village isolated from the main current of art activity, working with material until then little exploited, and setting themselves up as an exhibiting society stirred the imagination of critical reviewers and writers of art." In an interview with University of New Mexico graduate student Dorothy Skousen Black in 1959, Adams said that TSA meetings were uproarious and aesthetics were rarely discussed. Though individuals in the group feuded occasionally, they immediately united if attacked from without, and they were close, generous friends.

The early artists maintained a simple but gracious lifestyle. They set up attractive homes with distinguished furnishings and had plentiful household help. It was not Bohemia, but a frontier outpost of middle-class form and propriety that they established among themselves, similar to that of military officers of that era sent to some remote army post.

We see the artists in old photographs, painting in their studios still wearing white shirts and ties. Their life, we read in their accounts and letters, was pleasantly social. They shared dinners, bridge games, and conversational evenings. They liked to go fishing in streams of primeval beauty in a sportsman's paradise. But mostly they worked hard day after day on their art. When they opted for Taos, they left behind the many conveniences of modern cities in exchange for the quiet inspiration of the Taos valley.

In this scenic, remote area whose people were so ethnically distinctive, the cultures of the town and the pueblo had the patina of age. But it was all fresh material to the artists, and they were intoxicated by their discovery.

Blumenschein, in a much quoted explanation, wrote: "We were ennuied with the hackneyed subject matter of thousands of painters; windmills in a Dutch landscape; Brittany peasants with sabots; French roads lined with Normandy poplars, lady in negligee reclining on a sumptuous divan; lady gazing in mirror; lady powdering her nose; etc., etc. We felt the need of a stimulating subject. This, and the nature of youth, brought us to the west" (*El Palacio*, May 1926).

Blumenschein was blessed with a wit and ease of writing that has given us the best picture of his Taos experience and that of his friends. In his introduction for Laura Bickerstaff's book *Pioneer Artists of Taos*, one of the few books on the early Taos painters, Blumenschein wrote: "We all drifted into Taos like skilled hands looking for a good steady job. We found it, as it grew into a joyous inspiration to produce and give to the deepest extent of each man's own calibre. We lived only to paint. And that is what happens to every artist who passes this way."

Taos represented an aspect of western America that had captured the imagination of the country. As the Industrial Revolution roared ahead, those trapped in eastern cities were curious about the fading romance of Indian life in the distant west. The artists themselves were caught up in this feeling of romance.

The first artists of Taos were conservative, academically oriented painters. To begin with, some were commercial illustrators who attempted to paint what they saw with faithful, though romantic, exactitude. At first, the Indian motif dominated their work, but in later years they painted most everything, including flowers and landscapes. The international reputation of the older men rested on more than just their Indian paintings. They were not in the flush of youth when they arrived, but seasoned artists whose careers were already mature.

Dorothy Black theorized that the artists were in revolt against Impressionism, studio painting, and New York. She wrote in her fascinating master's thesis: "There was the common desire to adapt the long, bold brushstrokes and the bright colors of Post-Impressionism to the American landscape and people .... The landscape, adobe buildings, the colorful people, Indians, Spanish, Mexican, cowboys, and mountaineers created a strange world .... This milieu was ideal for the artistic temper of the time."

Black aptly quoted E. P. Richardson's *Painting in America:* "The compelling impulse of these men was a desire to paint the Indians, the noble landscape, and the burning sun of New Mexico as something uniquely American and rich in artistic significance. They found their subject in Taos as the painter-illustrators of the Eight found theirs in New York City."

The Taos Church, before modern reconstruction gave it two towers. Fenn Galleries Ltd.

Young Taos model. Bert Phillips Collection. Fenn Galleries Ltd.

Dancers at the Taos Pueblo. Fenn Galleries Ltd.

THERE IS DRAMA in the lives of these pioneers, but it is largely biographical rather than aesthetic in nature. Thus *The Legendary Artists of Taos* is concerned more with their humanness than with an analysis of their work. The early artists of Taos produced solid, even hauntingly memorable paintings, but they did not innovate. Cubism, Fauvism, and the quickly developing spearheads of modernism—abstraction and expressionism—did not really affect the first wave of artists in Taos.

Adams, trying to define what it was that held them together as a group, wrote: "In seeking some quality common to all of these eight (the TSA prior to the arrival of Hennings and Adams) individuals who reacted differently to the stimulus of the physical environment and the human life it embraced, I think I might say it was love; love that had in it elements of reverence for the awe-inspiring grandeur of the mountains, expanse of cultivated fields and desert, and the simple 'rightness' of 'belonging' that characterizes the Indians and the Spanish-American inhabitants of the Valley" (*New Mexico Quarterly*, Winter 1951).

The members of the TSA were not the only artists who came to live in Taos. Other stories besides those of the pioneers are part of the Taos history, and many of them are included in this book. When Andrew Dasburg arrived, he brought with him the excitement and turmoil of European revolutionary art. His visit affected the work of some artists who were already in Taos, notably Higgins, and attracted others, such as Adams, as followers. So, taking together the members of the TSA and those who lived in Taos but were not members, the broader picture of the Taos art colony is that of a diverse group of artists who reacted to the area with similar emotions, expressed in personal styles of realism.

To place the early artists of Taos in perspective, it is best to fit them into the western tradition that continues today in the work of the Cowboy Artists of America and the National Academy of Western Art, among others. A wave of popular interest in western art is currently sweeping the country, propelling a revival in the market for and curiosity about the art of the early Taos art colony. It is therefore appropriate now to rediscover the artists who created it, to learn their stories and enjoy their work, and perhaps to envy them their special time and place.

THE FOUNDING PIONEERS

The Taos Society of Artists. Top row (left to right): Walter Ufer, Herbert "Buck" Dunton, Victor Higgins, Kenneth Adams. Middle row: Joseph Henry Sharp, E. Martin Hennings, Eanger Irving Couse, Oscar Berninghaus. Bottom row: Bert Geer Phillips, Ernest Blumenschein. Photo courtesy Kibbey Couse.

JOSEPH HENRY SHARP
Dedicated Observer

PEOPLE REPEATEDLY describe Joseph Henry Sharp as lovable. A small man, with a trim Van Dyke beard, a neat mustache, and twinkly eyes behind steel-rimmed glasses, he is remembered as cheerful although he became totally deaf early in childhood.

Sharp is credited with prompting the art colony of Taos. In 1883 he was on a painting trip near Santa Fe when he first heard about the remote pueblo village—but he did not actually see it then. Instead, from Santa Fe, Sharp continued traveling to California and up the coast to visit the northwestern tribes. On that trip he made sketches of the Utes, Shoshones, and Klikitats.

In 1893 Sharp again visited the Territory of New Mexico, but this time he spent the summer in Taos. He was deeply moved by the majesty of the landscape; more impressive to him still were the Pueblo and the Taos Indians, whose culture had remained stable despite 300 years of Spanish rule. The multistoried pueblo had been standing on the site for centuries prior to the arrival of Spanish explorers in the mid-16th century.

Such endurance meant to Sharp that there was less urgency about capturing the Taos culture on canvas than there was about painting the other more vulnerable Indian cultures, particularly that of the Northern Plains tribes. So Sharp spent much of the next few years on the plains, but he retained his interest in Taos.

In 1895 Sharp was in Europe studying in the ateliers of Jean Paul Laurens and Benjamin Constant. Also in Paris at the time were Ernest L. Blumenschein and Bert Phillips. When Sharp met them and vividly described Taos, he excited their imagination. They eventually found their way to Taos and were identified with the village ever after.

Joseph Henry Sharp enjoyed a blossoming career even before he saw Taos, and he continued to paint throughout his long life. He was born of Irish-American parents on September 27, 1859, in Bridgeport, Ohio. Since his father was an amateur painter, while Sharp was still a child, he felt an urge to become an artist too. Orphaned at 13, he went to live with his aunt in Cincinnati. Money was scarce because his father—a merchant by trade—had lost a comfortable fortune before he died, so by day young Henry worked as a waterboy and in a nail factory in order to pay for art lessons at night.

Sharp was an avid student, first at the McMicken School of Design and then at the Cincinnati Art Academy. When he was 22, he spent a year in Antwerp studying under Charles Verlat. On a trip to Europe in 1886 he studied in Munich under Carl Marr at the Royal Academy, where he met the American academician Frank Duveneck, who had been on the faculty of the Cincinnati Art Academy for a number of years, and traveled with him on a tour of museums in Italy and Spain. There Sharp copied Goya, Velasquez, and El Greco at the Prado Museum in Madrid. He kept those paintings in his living room, and eventually moved them to his Taos studio.

Sharp was a gifted draftsman and an accurate, objective observer, and the human form was his forte. For ten years, from 1892 to 1902, he taught life drawing and portraiture at the Cincinnati Art Academy. During those same years he began spending time following his passion, the study of American Indian tribes in their own homes.

Just as George Catlin (with whom Sharp is often compared) became obsessed with interest in American Indians after seeing a delegation of Western Indians passing through Philadelphia in 1824, Sharp remembered eagerly watching the Indians who visited near his early childhood farm home in West Virginia in 1865, when he was six. From that time on, their dignity and natural beauty became his consuming interest. People writing about Sharp have stressed his human appeal.

In "An Indian Painter in the West," an article that appeared in *El Palacio* in 1922, Laura A. Davies wrote: "Seldom has there been an artist, historian or writer who has tracked the savage to his lair, lived with him and won his confidence in the thorough way that Mr. Sharp has done. He is a typical American, full of tact, energy and ingenuity. He is intensely human and has always treated the Indian as a brother, and as a result has never had an unpleasant experience in all his intimate relations with him. It has often been said that Landseer painted dogs so well because he loved them. The same might be said with equal truth of Sharp's Indians. He peeps into their hearts. His vivid imagination sees things from their viewpoint. He feels the thrill of things that thrill his subjects and so he puts the living spirit, not merely the technically exact portrait, upon his canvas."

Sharp managed to combine his desire to paint Indians with his need to support himself and his new bride, Addie Byram. In the summers he traveled, visiting Indians in the West; in the winters he was in Cincinnati, on the faculty of the art academy. He also interspersed those years with European trips.

Cincinnati was far from a backwoods town. It was a noted art center where Sharp was considered a top-ranking painter whose reputation was enhanced by his Indian paintings. On his travels among the Indians, he took copious notes on the ceremonies and lifestyles he observed. As he told Ina Sizer Cassidy in an interview for *New Mexico Magazine*, "I was always interested, even as a small boy, I guess it was Fenimore Cooper who first attracted me to the Indian. It was the romance of youth, of boyhood I suppose. But boys always did like Indians. Then when I came to know them I liked them for themselves. Perhaps they attracted me as subjects to paint because of their important historical value as First Americans. There is something very intriguing about 'First Americans.' Then the color of their costumes and dances, this no less attracted me. Their color is glorious and so belongs to them and to their country."

unting Son, 1926. Oil, 16 x 20" (41 x 51 cm). Collection Mr. and Mrs. Gerald P. Peters.

Evening Camp, Blackfoot Reservation. *Oil on board, 5 x 8¼" (13 x 21 cm). Fenn Galleries Ltd., Santa Fe.*

Our Garden. *Oil, 16 x 20" (41 x 51 cm). Fenn Galleries Ltd., Santa Fe.*

THE FIRST PROTRACTED effort Sharp made to study Indians was among the tribes of Montana. He adapted a shepherd's wagon to his need for a studio by making a skylight of sheet mica and christened it "The Prairie Dog." From this portable spot he painted the site of the Battle of Little Big Horn, only 25 years after the massacre.

Sharp was a gritty, brave, and determined fellow. He returned to the site annually; and, in 1902, he had a log cabin built adjacent to the reservation. Two years later he had his studio built and when it was ready he sent out amusing invitations to its opening. The studio is still intact, just beyond the Crow Agency. Sharp's paintings of the Crow, Sioux, and Blackfeet are among the finest he ever did.

Laura Davies wrote in *El Palacio:* "Speaking of the portrait of a chief prominent in Custer's battle, he [Sharp] said, 'Note the quizzical half-smile on that Indian. He was one of my early subjects in the Sioux Reservations. He never could see why I should pay him two dollars a day just to sit and let me look at him. He used to joke with me about it and tell me he thought I must be crazy and then every once in a while he would smile, and I knew just what was making him laugh inside. That's why I caught the expression and put it on canvas.'"

California, too, was a base for Sharp and he maintained a studio there for years. In 1902 Phoebe Hearst, William Randolph Hearst's mother, bought 80 of his Indian portraits and offered him a contract to paint 15 more works of representative Indian people a year for five years. The collection, now the property of the University of California at Berkeley, totals 95, so we can assume the agreement was discontinued after a year. Nonetheless, that is an enormous collection of work by a single artist. This sale gave Sharp the financial freedom to travel and paint, rather than stay on the faculty in Cincinnati.

After 1902, a rhythmic pattern developed in Sharp's life: he painted among the Plains Indians and he painted among the Taos Indians. Oddly enough he was in the north during the harshest winter weather, and in Taos during more benign weather. While in Taos he would use Pueblo Indian models to create his paintings of Plains Indians, relying on his notes to supplement his memories.

In Taos, Henry and Addie at first lived in rented quarters, but in 1909 he bought a place on Kit Carson Road that included a former Penitente *morada*, a chapel that once belonged to the Penitente sect of flagellants. It was even thought that the historic old adobe had bloodstains on the walls from their flagellation rites. Sharp hung his early paintings in the morada but otherwise did not use it.

Carved beams across the high ceilings, a large fireplace, and the Sharp collection of truly outstanding Indian artifacts made the Sharp residence a most attractive dwelling. Its grounds were enclosed by long walls with a bell left over from its days as a chapel, hung in an archway. Sharp's home adjoined Couse's. Both homes had been owned by the Christian Brothers, who ran a school and a monastery there. After the death of the Sharps, his property reverted to the Couse family.

In 1913 Addie Sharp died. Two years later Sharp went back to the Midwest and married her sister Louise. His second marriage lasted for over 40 years until his death in 1953. (Louise died six years later.) The Sharps were a devoted couple who depended on each other entirely, as they had no children.

The same year of his marriage to Louise, Sharp built a separate studio behind his home. The garden around the place was known as one of the loveliest in Taos. There he raised delphinium, poppies, phlox, and Shasta daisies. Iris and dahlias grew around the sundial and birdbath. On the terraces there were willows and fruit trees. Sharp often painted still lifes of flowers from his own flowerbeds.

Regina Tatum Cooke, artist and writer of Taos, remembers that she used to stroll along the road past Sharp's garden and find him sitting there at his easel, wearing his battered hat as always. With the help of a little pad he always carried and his skill at lip reading, he would chat with her. She described him as a contented, energetic, and delightful person.

Kibbey W. Couse, son of E. Irving Couse, wrote this amusing account of his parents' friends, the Sharps, in the *Taos News* (September 12, 1968): "It was a tradition of the Couses to have the Sharps over twice a year for a formal dinner. There was much instruction from Mrs. Sharp as to dry toast, lettuce, tea, etc., during the week before this event. When the evening arrived, the Sharps always forgot their troubles (with indigestion) and gorged themselves on good roast beef, baked potatoes and all the fixings, including a good wine.

The next morning Mrs. Couse would ask Alois Liebert, who was Sharp's right-hand man, how they had survived the night and he would invariably say, 'Fine! Fine! They never slept better!'"

In 1933 the Sharps traveled to China and later to Hawaii. But wherever he was, the painting schedule Sharp followed was simply to work all day, every day of the week, until the light faded. As a result, he turned out a volume of paintings with a wide diversity in quality.

J.H. Sharp on location near his mobile outdoor studio, a converted shepherd's wagon he called "The Prairie Dog." The Lucinda Martin Iliff Collection, Kit Carson Memorial Foundation, Taos.

Landscape with Creek. *Oil, 24 x 36" (61 x 91 cm). Fenn Galleries Ltd., Santa Fe.*

Peonies. *30 x 36" (76 x 91 cm). Private collection.*

IN TODAY'S LIVELY market, the paintings Sharp did of the Crows and Sioux are in great demand. These impressions of grasslands, tepee villages, braves, and squaws are delicately painted in pastel shades with a feathery touch. With this shorthand style, Sharp presented scenes honestly and aesthetically. They still provide us an intimate closeup of a culture as it was in its innocence. Sharp was fully aware of the transcience of culture, of its vulnerability.

Portraits painted by Sharp faithfully recorded the features of numerous tribal chiefs. One of Sharp's models was the Sioux Chief Flat Iron, whom he painted at least five times. They became close friends. Sharp's deafness, his courtliness, and gentle, unthreatening manner gave him a rapport with his Indian subjects. He spent so many years studying the Indian with empathy that his canvases reflect his understanding and there is an emotional undertone to them. The objectivity of a reporter inspired his work, but Sharp did not lose sight of artistic demands. His compositions were sound—never exciting or innovative, but pleasing. Sharp was an accomplished academic painter, and as such he could capture the form and feature of his models admirably well. His portraits and traditional figure pieces were solid, classic oil paintings.

Sharp sometimes posed his models in firelight and these paintings are much in demand today. In "An Indian Painter of the West," Laura A. Davies described the scene: "When the cool days of fall begin to arrive he has a roaring fire built in the big fireplace in his Taos studio. He groups his figures around it in their natural attitudes at their familiar tasks or pastime and the stage is set for a masterpiece."

Sharp never used Indians to suit a painting; on the contrary, he used painting to serve as a record of the Indians. In an unpublished research paper, *Joseph Henry Sharp/Indian Painter and Conformist,* Vivian Kline makes this statement: "He wished to record the Indian as an ethnic phenomenon, a way of life which he knew was disappearing." She strengthens her theory by pointing out that Sharp's first major sales were to the Department of Anthropology at the University of California and the Bureau of Ethnology of the Smithsonian Institution, and that they were valued for their accuracy rather than their artistry, initially. A tone that ran through the many critical reviews of his paintings was one that stressed their historical value. In his annual shows at the Traxel or Kreimer Galleries in Cincinnati, Sharp featured painting after painting of certain models who became familiar to the viewers. Ms. Kline also presents arguments to substantiate her view that Sharp's success rests on his conformity to the values of his time. He, like Roosevelt, was able to capture the interest of a wide following for whom the vanishing wilderness and the Indians who lived in it were a romantic attraction.

However, there was more to Sharp's work than dry fact, as you can perceive in his *Taos Indian Portrait,* owned by the Museum of New Mexico. In this painting, the remote expression of the sitter dominates his impressive costume. The division of lights and darks as strong diagonals alleviates the static pose. A path of lights in the edging of the robe links face, hands, and decorative details such as the feathers and beads in a deft fashion.

Taos Indian Irrigating His Corn is a narrow vertical painting of a full standing figure, balanced by the corn stalks in the field and the red earth of the little irrigation channel at the feet of the Indian. Here the charm of the painting is in the fresh, glazed colors that carry the bright, sunny impression of a naturalistic closeup. Bright, clear color is not typical of the Taos artists of the period.

Sharp's floral still lifes often appear on the market and, though uneven in quality, there are some that glow with refreshing hues and have graceful compositions.

Sharp was never elected to the National Academy, although his style was appropriate. He did win some fine prizes, though: a silver medal at the Pan American Exposition in Buffalo, New York, in 1901; and a gold medal at the Panama-California Exposition in San Diego, in 1915. He was a founder of the Taos Society of Artists, a member of the Salmagundi Club, the Society of Western Artists, the Artists' Guild of Chicago, the Duveneck Society of Cincinnati, the Print Makers Club of Los Angeles, and the California Art Club.

Eleven portraits of Indian chiefs are in the collection of the Smithsonian Institution, bought from a Washington, D.C. show in 1901. Other major collections of his work are at the Butler Museum in Youngstown, Ohio, the Cincinnati Museum of Art, and the Thomas Gilcrease Institute of Art in Tulsa, Oklahoma.

His honors came in the popular acceptance of his work (he made more money than any of the other Taos artists), the many sales he made to important museum and private collections, and the successful realization of his lifetime goals.

He summarized his feelings in this statement (quoted in *El Palacio,* May 1926): "In past years I have seen so many things and made studies that probably no other living artist ever saw, such as the Tobacco Dance, Graves, Burials, etc., that if I do not paint them no one ever will."

Joseph Henry Sharp died in Pasadena, California, on August 29, 1953, just a few days before his 94th birthday.

BERT GEER PHILLIPS
Taos Romantic

The broken wheel, 1898. Courtesy private collection.

OTHER ARTISTS WERE painting in New Mexico before Bert Phillips rolled in on a wagon along with Ernest L. Blumenschein in the fall of 1898. Worthington Whittredge was in the state just after the Civil War; Thomas Moran painted the pueblos in the 1880s, about the time Joseph Henry Sharp first traveled to Santa Fe; and Frederic Remington made several trips through the state in the same decade. They came and they painted pictures that were conveyers of beauty and romance to viewers in the East, but none of them stayed during that early period. Bert Phillips did stay. He knew immediately that Taos was to be his permanent home. In the May 1926 issue of *El Palacio*, Ernest L. Blumenschein wrote: "Phillips is the foundation on which the Taos group built!"

Phillips was a well-bred Yankee of dignified bearing with a long face, high forehead, and a mobile, expressive mouth. Of all those artists who formed the Taos Society of Artists, Phillips was the one most deeply involved in his personal life with the town and the pueblo. He never lost his romantic view of Taos.

For Phillips, that first fall season passed in a delirium of enthusiastic hours painting the area with Blumenschein. The two men avidly absorbed the atmosphere. They were good friends who had met in Paris in 1895 as fellow students under Constant and Laurens at the Académie Julien, when Joseph Henry Sharp intrigued them with his vivid description of Taos. He advised them to do as he did and paint the Indian before he disappeared. Back in the States, Phillips shared a studio with Blumenschein for two years.

After Blumenschein returned from an illustration commission in Arizona and New Mexico with a contagious desire to return to the Southwest, he talked Phillips into joining him the following summer for a western painting trip to begin in Denver and extend into Mexico. Early in the summer of 1898 they arrived in Denver and bought a wagon, horses, and gear.

Bert Phillips wrote of this adventure in an account preserved in family correspondence and published by the *Taos News* in 1968: "About the greenest gringoes that ever struck the west, they did not know how to saddle a horse, much less hitch [one] up [to a wagon in] a livery stable. Blumy said, 'Now Phil, you get on one side and watch. I'll be on the other. Between the two of us we should learn how they put on the harness and hook up to the wagon. If we buy, we'll do the job ourselves tomorrow when we start, and they'll never know how green we are.'

"The next day, having purchased the complete outfit and 'hooked up,' they drove down Broadway and were soon out of town happily on their way when they were stopped by an old farmer, who scowled fiercely as he yelled: 'Hey! you fellers want to kill someone!' He left his team, came over, (and) angrily crossed the ends of the reins to each horse. ... The two artists camped and painted the red rocks of Deer Creek Canyon south of Denver for several months before they began the southward trek when the weather turned cooler. In the much-told tale of the broken wagon wheel near Questa, New Mexico, the two men described their fated digression to Taos as follows: After casting lots, Bert Phillips remained behind to guard the wagon while Blumenschein took the wheel to the nearest blacksmith for repairs. When he got back to Phillips on the canyon rim three days later, he had already become entranced by Taos.

Ever afterward both men felt as though they were led to the village and that they had shared a mystical experience. They abandoned their trip to Mexico, sold their wagon, horses, and gear, rented a studio in Taos and painted through the fall months. Blumenschein's commitments in New York forced him to leave, but Phillips decided to remain. Luckily some paintings Phillips sent back with Blumenschein were bought by the O'Brian Gallery in Chicago, so he could afford to stay.

Twining Canyon. Oil, 36 x 30″ (91 x 76 cm). McAdoo Galleries, Inc. Woodrow Wilson Fine Arts.

HILLIPS WAS 30 years old then, a well-prepared artist who no longer felt the need for European academies. At the age of 16 he had left his home in Hudson, New York for five years of study at the Art Students League and the National Academy of Design. Afterward he had painted for a living, spending several more years in New York before traveling to Europe. In 1894 he painted in England and then moved on to Paris where he later met Blumenschein.

The West captured Phillip's imagination early in his life when he found an arrowhead, lost by some forgotten Mohegan. Kit Carson was the artist's boyhood hero. His mental imagery was created by James Fenimore Cooper's books. Before he ever saw the West, Phillips enjoyed a successful career painting western illustrations. His models were a half-Sioux and cowboys: he painted them in western landscapes invented from research. It was natural for him to become infatuated by the West when he finally saw it.

Bert Phillips knew his career could easily continue in Taos, and after he settled there he became the mainstay of the Taos artists group as it grew. The others were there only in the summers for some years before settling in the village permanently. The year after he moved to Taos, Phillips courted and won the local doctor's sister, Rose Martin, who had come out for a visit from her native Pennsylvania. They were married in 1899. In their 54 years of a shared life, they had two children: a daughter Margaret and a son Ralph.

Phillips sent his work out on circuit shows with the Taos Society of Artists and to his Chicago and New York galleries. He was also a gracious host in his own studio, which he had set up as a gallery for frequent visitors. In those days there were no commercial galleries in Taos, and artists opened their studios for the tourists who made the effort to visit the region.

Phillips' studio, located just north of the plaza on a corner backed against the historic Governor Bent home, had formerly belonged to an old buffalo hunter. Its private garden was surrounded by a high adobe wall with a door to the road. Inside was a patio sheltered by an enclosing L-shaped portal, hung with Virginia creeper.

Regina Tatum Cooke relates an anecdote Phillips liked to tell: "As I was painting on the patio, two horsemen were riding by in the street and I heard them say 'You never know what you'll find behind these old walls.'"

The visitors to Phillips' home found not only gracious hospitality, but also Indian art worthy of a museum. Several features of the place were memorable. The studio itself had a high ceiling sloping up to a north window. In a showcase and on furniture, Phillips displayed his notable collection of Indian artifacts. There were pottery, beadwork, blankets, clothing, and weaponry in abundance. He was an early champion of the Indian. In an interview for the *Albuquerque Evening Herald*, (reported in *El Palacio*, May 24, 1919, p. 178), Phillips said of the Indians: "Their contribution to art has been invaluable. We come out here to learn from them and find an apparently inexhaustible store of beauty and originality. I have seen Indian rugs whose beauty of design, texture, and color were as fine as any Persian rug that has been woven. They are absolutely different in character, of course, but quite as valuable from an artistic standpoint."

In the early years, despite the poorly lit, awkward conditions, Phillips painted the Taos Indians in their own pueblo homes, and he came to be their trusted friend.

They invited him to try his skill in their foot races on San Geronimo Day, celebrated each September 30. Such an invitation is an unusual courtesy to extend an outsider, and Phillips was proud of the honor. He was an outdoorsman at heart and a good runner. Phillips ran lightly on his toes and won. The Indians, who ran more solidly on their whole foot, asked him to take off his shoes. They thought he had put a feather in them to make him so speedy.

On the basis of friendship, Phillips became a champion of Taos Pueblo Indian causes. In 1904, through his unflagging and intelligent efforts, the right to the mountainous watershed adjacent to the pueblo—land traditionally belonging to the Indians—was restored to them. Phillips had a friend in Washington, Vernon Bailey, who was the chief of the Bureau of Biology, and it was to him that Phillips turned in this venture. When the government created a national forest in the mountains surrounding Taos, it was Phillips' suggestion that it be named the Kit Carson National Forest, and so it was.

Phillip's painting on location. The Lucinda Martin Iliff Collection, Kit Carson Memorial Foundation, Taos.

Kit Carson's scout with Bert Phillips' daughter. Fenn Galleries, Ltd., Santa Fe.

Bert Phillips painting My Patio. *(See painting in color on page 54.) Photo private collection.*

Taos Mountain. *Oil, 8 x 10′ (20 x 25 cm). Collection Edwin B. Nelsons.*

WHEN PHILLIPS BECAME the victim of serious eye trouble that prevented him from painting his models in their homes, his Indian friends created a raised corner in his studio that was an authentic segment of a pueblo room, complete with a corner fireplace built in the traditional beehive shape, a niche for an artifact in the wall, vigas (beams) on the ceiling, and walls of adobe. Here his models would sit stoically and immobile for hours at a time. In the course of these shared hours, Phillips collected numerous tales and he became a most informed and delightful raconteur.

His eye problem finally completely interfered with his painting and he had to supplement his income some other way. For four years he worked as a forest ranger, the very first one employed by the newly created Kit Carson National Forest. As he rode the trails by horseback, he was constantly aware of the vistas, the stuff of his art. He became, for this period, a creator of mental images. This freed him to a certain extent from the viewpoint of a faithful renderer. When his eyesight improved, he returned to full-time painting with a heightened sense of romance.

Phillips did not secure the esteemed national position that fell to Blumenschein and others, but it is unlikely that he sought to compete with the same fervor as the rest. His style, described by Van Deren Coke as "lyrical," was sweet rather than powerful, reflecting his feelings of identification with his Indian theme, and his contentment.

Phillips was aided by his own reputation and by the loyal friendship of the other Taos artists. Shortly after he was made an honorary member of the Society of Western Artists, in a letter dated January 12, 1902, Oscar E. Berninghaus wrote him: "You seem to be doing very well in Chicago. I heard offhand that your pictures are bringing three and four hundred dollars. I hope the [sic] goodness it is true because they certainly ought to. I know Cincinnati is loud in praise of your work but wait untill [sic] the coming exhibition of the S of W A when it reaches St. Louis . . . I am going to push you all I can here."

Yet in spite of some early economic highpoints, Phillips somehow missed out on earning a proper amount of money for his work. For a time he sent small Indian portraits, excellently painted in the tradition of the masters, to his New York dealer. But he received only $50 for them while the dealer resold them for $500; one was even bought by Frederic Remington. Had Phillips been more aggressive and traveled more on his own behalf, he could have rectified his status; but he rarely made the effort.

During the '20s he was included in the mural contract to paint lunettes for the new capitol of Missouri at Jefferson City. He also painted murals for the Polk County Court House of Des Moines, Iowa, the courthouse of Taos, and the San Marcos Hotel in Chandler, Arizona.

Phillips seemed to view the Indian as a classic symbol representing innocence, grace, and purity. In his painting titles he reveals a poetic side to his nature—*Symphony of the Aspen Forest* and *Exhaltation Song to the Moon Mother*, for example. His work also had a manneristic quality, a weightlessness and dreaminess that seemed to grow more pronounced with time. At his best, he captured the color and appeal of his subjects with charm and an obvious affection.

Phillips was asked to contribute a statement for the catalog of a show held at Babcock Galleries, New York, later republished in *El Palacio* (July 1920): "Sometimes I ask myself why I remain away from the "Land of Civilization" but never before have I tried to formulate a reply. I have simply been content to stay on. The charm of the great stretches of mountain and plains and the interest of their inhabitants is never ending. As I visit their villages and talk with my Indian friends, I see and hear the young bucks wrapped in their white blankets standing on the bridge singing a love song in the moonlight and I feel the romance of youth, so the answer comes as I write and I believe that it is the romance of this great pure aired land that makes the most lasting impression on my mind and heart."

The title "Pioneer Artist" was a source of pride to Phillips. By his performance as an artist, a friend of the Indians, permanent resident, guide to countless visitors, and entertaining, knowledgeable story-teller, Bert Phillips filled his role with distinction. He died in 1956, three years after his beloved Rose, in San Diego, California, following a stroke.

Bert Phillips' studio in Taos. High-rising roof at back held large north window. Fenn Galleries Ltd., Santa Fe.

ERNEST L. BLUMENSCHEIN
Intellect and Growth

IS FRIENDS CALLED him Blumy. Wiry and witty, he was a determined and energetic artist. If the Taos art colony has its "Legend of Creation," its writer and co-hero was Ernest L. Blumenschein.

Laura Bickerstaff quoted one version of Blumenschein's legend in *Pioneer Artists of Taos*. In this account, Blumy tells of hearing about Taos from Henry Sharp while he was studying in Paris. After returning to the States, Blumy was given an assignment to do an illustration for *McClure's Magazine*. To complete it, he had to make a trip to the Southwest. On his return he convinced Bert Phillips to join him on a trip west the following summer. In Denver, the two greenhorns bought a wagon, some gear and two horses, intending to paint and camp their way to Mexico.

On September 3, 1898, as they climbed a hill south of Questa, New Mexico, their wagon slipped in a rut and a rear wheel collapsed. As Dorothy Skousen Black later reported in her unpublished M.A. thesis, Blumenschein said: "We flipped a three-dollar gold piece to see which of us stayed on the mountain with the outfit and one horse. It was my fortune to get the task of carrying that wheel on horseback to Taos. . . . Vividly I recall the discomfort of lugging that unwieldly load with no relief in sight, no wagon going my way, no hope to ease sore muscles until I reached Taos (20 miles away), the dim picture of which I had made in imagination from Sharp's slight description.

"But Sharp had not painted for me the land or the mountains and plains and clouds. No artist had ever recorded the New Mexico I was now seeing. . . . I was receiving, under rather painful circumstances, the first great unforgettable inspiration of my life. . . . I realized I was getting my own impressions from nature, seeing it for the first time with my own eyes, uninfluenced by the art of any man." His words, well chosen as they were, could give only a glimpse of the emotions aroused in him by the Taos Valley, the Spanish village, and the Indian pueblo as he first saw them glowing in the brilliance of autumn sunshine.

The initial passion he felt then at discovering such dramatic subject matter never left him, though at 24, Blumenschein had already enough sophisticated experience behind him to be able to recognize clearly what this area could mean to him. Dorothy Skousen Black quotes him as saying: "When I came to this valley, for the first time in my life, I saw whole paintings right before my eyes. Everywhere I looked I saw paintings perfectly organized, ready to paint."

Born in Pittsburgh, Pennsylvania, on May 26, 1874, Blumenschein was raised in Dayton, Ohio, by cultivated people of German descent. His father was a conductor of choruses, a composer, and an organist. Blumenschein was a talented violinist who had won a scholarship to the Cincinnati College of Music at the age of 17. A year later he realized his true goal was to become a painter, and he left for New York. But during his years of study at the Art Students League, he also played first violin under visiting conductor-composer Anton Dvorak.

From New York, the young artist went to Paris and, following the classic path of development, enrolled at the Académie Julien. At age 22, he returned to New York and immediately began painting illustrations for some of the finest magazines in circulation, such as *Scribner's*, *Harper's*, and *Century*, in addition to *McClure's Magazine*. Despite his enthralling trip to Taos in 1898, Blumenschein went back to Paris for further study. It is a comment on the preparation he demanded of himself that he continued to study after winning commercial acceptance.

In 1900 Blumenschein returned to the States and painted the illustrations for Charles A. Eastman's *Indian Boyhood* during a visit to Taos. He wrote in a letter to a business associate that summer, revealing with youthful ardor his poetic response to the area: "I am wildly enthusiastic over my surroundings. I live in a little adobe town built up by a tiny stream which cuts through the desert and loses itself in the painted canyon of the Rio Grande. Everything about me is inspiring me to work. . . .

"Music is all I miss. But we have that in the storms that time all the instruments of nature to noble harmonies, and in the quiet nights that fill a man's soul with a calm rhythm in accord with all that is serene and beautiful.

"The cottonwoods and the pines are the violins, the sweeping grass of the Prairie plays the cello, a plunging brook is a silver flute, the quivering aspen leaves a tremulous oboe, and the Master Musician blows through the canons from far across the desert."

Portrait of the Family. *Oil on canvas, 47 x 45½″ (119 x 116 cm). Collection Museum of Fine Arts, Museum of New Mexico, Santa Fe.*

(Opposite page) 1939 July Fiesta Parade. Blumenschein and Phillips reenacting their own legend of the broken wagon wheel and their discovery of Taos. Fenn Galleries Ltd., Santa Fe.

I N THE CLINTON P. ANDERSON Collection of Zimmerman
Library, University of New Mexico, there is a personal
copy of *Indian Boyhood* that the late Senator had sent
to Blumenschein, asking him to inscribe it. On the fly-
leaf in his own handwriting is a lengthy description of this
commission:

"Being a good ballplayer, I was enabled to get close to the
young Sioux, who took me with the team for games with
clubs of neighboring cities and towns. As we drove over the
prairies to and from our games the boys seemed happy, as
they sang almost incessantly. . . .

"In addition to my travels with the ballclub, Dr. Eastman, a delightful man, often took me in his buggy as he
made calls on the sick about the large reservation. We usually carried shotguns, and stopped to hunt whenever we
flushed a covy of prairie chickens. And the wild game was a
great help to the table of an Indian reservation. The Doctor
told me many stories not quite appropriate for this book,
legends concerning the characteristics of wild creatures,
and sometimes of man. And always on my trips with ball-
players or Doctor, I carried my sketchbook.

"After two months of this interesting life, I began work
on my illustrations, which took me four months before com-
pletion. *Indian Boyhood* has been selling for forty years
and will live much longer, because of its sincere quality and
the charming simplicity of its style. Ernest L. Blumenschein."

Blumenschein worked and studied in Paris from 1902 to
1908. After an illustration assignment he completed for
McClure's (Love of Life) was extravagantly praised, he pro-
posed to and married Mary Shepard Greene, a better-
known artist than he was at the time, and five years his sen-
ior. Mary Shepard Greene had been in Paris for 17 years
and was recognized for both illustrations and exhibition
paintings. She had won prizes at the salons in Paris and in
New York where she became an Associate of the National
Academy. The Blumenschein marriage, both an inspiration
and a source of mental anguish to the couple, lasted
throughout their long lives. They had one surviving child,
Helen Greene Blumenschein, born in 1909 in New York
City. She is also an accomplished artist (see page 31).

A revealing painting, *Portrait of the Family* (page 29) is
owned by the Museum of Fine Arts in Santa Fe, New Mexico. Painted when Helen was four years old, it gives a psy-
chological insight into the early years of the Blumenschein
marriage. Mary Greene Blumenschein's mother had to be
convinced that her daughter had made a proper choice for a
husband. After the couple lost their first child, a son,
Helen's frail health was a concern. By Helen's fourth year,
the family felt relief that she was getting stronger. In the
portrait Helen sits on her grandmother's lap, Mary Greene
Blumenschein is shown with her palette, and Ernest Blumenschein has pictured himself with his violin. Behind the
figures he has painted a symbolic Victory. With this painting he was propitiating his mother-in-law, as though he
were saying he would not compete with her daughter, and
that they could, after all, have a healthy child. The early
years were the time when Ernest Blumenschein did the ac-
commodating; later his wife made concessions to her husband's career. Perhaps it was her way of showing her grat-
itude as well as her commitment.

For a decade, the two Blumenscheins were involved in
book and magazine illustrations. After 1909, they lived in
New York and shared a studio where they collaborated on a
number of illustrations, she doing the women and he doing
the men.

Before leaving Paris, Ernest Blumenschein had illustrated Jack London's first book, *Love of Life.* In the next ten
years he illustrated other books by Stephen Crane, Willa
Cather, Joseph Conrad, and Booth Tarkington. Between
commissions he painted, entered competitions, and taught
at the Art Students League.

For a decade Blumenschein spent winters in New York
and summers in Taos, but to his wife, whose taste was
formed in the sophistication of Parisian salons, Taos
sounded too primitive. She remained in New York with
Helen while her husband rented living space in the village
of Taos. The oils he did during the summers were often entered in competitions the following season.

Afternoon of a Sheepherder. *Oil, 28 x 50" (71 x 127 cm). Fenn Galleries, Ltd., Santa Fe.*

THOUGH BLUMENSCHEIN'S sales of exhibition paintings were often erratic in those years, he felt a strong desire to drop commercial work and paint only what he wished. Luckily for him, in 1917 his wife came into her inheritance of money and a house in Brooklyn, where they were able to live for two years.

Ernest Blumenschein was torn between his devotion to his family and his enormous need to be in the Southwest. His wife and daughter were with him briefly in 1915, but the living conditions he found satisfactory were unacceptable to Mary. The Blumenschein papers reveal a poignant loneliness, love, and anger mixed with the usual domestic trivia in a spate of letters that passed between the couple in the first half of 1919, after Mary agreed to move to Taos. Her decision (which she could not bring herself to tell him until he had left New York) gave him the anticipated pleasure of at last sharing his love for the Southwest with his cherished Mary and Helen.

He wrote to her of his feelings, saying: "You've added to the dignity of my name by your good capable art work. You've decorated the house with a charmante petite-fille, you are the class of lady a man is always proud to show off as his'n. And you are a pleasing sight for the eye to feed upon." His letter touched his wife deeply, but she did make a proviso to her move, insisting that he find a suitable house.

Helen Blumenschein described the family's home in Taos in an unpublished article as follows: "We lived on Ledoux Street. Our house, built of adobe, was strung out in a straight line. Father bought four rooms of this place from 'Buck' Dunton who had settled there several years before. As time went on and the old occupants on either side of us died, we would purchase their rooms, until finally we had 11 rooms, enough to supply a studio for each of us and have bedrooms for our summer guests."

The Blumenschein house was a gathering place for shared dinners and story-telling. Reluctant as she had been to live in the isolated village, Mary Blumenschein brought her gracious manners and taste to Taos. The impact of this talented couple was intense in the clannish community. Their intellectual and aesthetic judgment helped establish a standard which was identified with the early Taos artists.

As Helen Blumenschein remembers Taos in the '20s: "It smelled of piñon smoke from the cooking and heating fires as we had no electricity, telephone, or plumbing. Going to the outhouse at -10° was something! Plowing through adobe clay after the spring thaw to walk to town and do the shopping was something else again. You had to shovel the snow off of the dirt roofs to prevent leaks and literally keep the home fires burning all day during the winter. All this physical effort kept us strong once we got over the first few years' hump."

Out of respect for her husband's needs, Mary Greene Blumenschein stopped painting in 1922, turning to jewelry design instead. Some of her distinctive pieces were sent on exhibition with her husband's work. It is significant that the Taos Art Society briefly had one woman member, Catherine Carter Critcher, an artist from Virginia. Yet Mary Greene Blumenshcein, already an Associate of the National Academy of Design, was never made a member of the local society founded by her husband and others in 1912.

Male pride was a marked characteristic of her father's nature as it was for many others of the period, Helen Blumenschein agreed, but her mother was actually responsible for staying out of the TSA. When she questioned her mother about it, she received the reply: "I do not believe it wise to have two Blumenscheins in the same society."

Mary Blumenschein's accommodation to her husband's career seemed to increase the happiness of her marriage. Both parents really found themselves in Taos. Their daughter believes her mother's work in jewelry and other designs was the finest she ever did, and her father's response to Taos after 1919 was to change his approach to his art. He adopted a brighter palette and he gave rein to an intuitive, mystical understanding of his Indian subjects, portraying not just their appearance but also their emotions. His work combined factual and imaginary elements with direct observation in nature, and from that inspiration he would add to his work, sometimes over a period of time. These later additions were intuitive, drawn from his experience and understanding of the subject.

THE RHYTHMS OF LIFE in Taos reflected the varied cultures of the village. The Spanish celebrated a seasonal calendar of Christian holidays. At Taos Pueblo, three miles from the central plaza, the indians held dances and relay races, depending on the season. Each September 30th, on San Geronimo Day, their celebration would start with foot races, followed by an Indian market and feast. In mid-afternoon the clown clan, called Chifonettis, who painted their bodies in black and white stripes, climbed a 50-foot (15m) pole to reach a bundle of booty and a dead sheep. Wintertime brought the Deer Dance and in summertime the Corn Dance was held. These colorful pageants were the stimulus for many of Blumenschein's paintings.

A Blumenschein *Deer Dance* is owned by the Gilcrease Institute of Art in Tulsa, Oklahoma, and Helen Blumenschein's story of that painting tells us something of the Blumenschein method: "The fire crackled at the campfire. Papa came back from his work that afternoon laughing because he had been doing a large 4' by 2½' vertical painting of aspens and in the foreground he had painted Adam and Eve walking out of the beautiful pristine forest. He had left his canvas for a short time and came back to find, as though the hand of the Lord had painted it, a flame coming up between the two figures. It turned out that a cow had come by and slapped its tail against the canvas. Father accentuated the flame with his brush and called the painting *Adam and Eve Leaving the Garden of Eden.* Some years later he took out Adam and Eve, replacing them with Deer Dancers: the two women were most effective coming out of the aspen forest."

For Helen, there were many hours of fishing, camping, and painting trips shared with her father (who called her Bill) and one of his favorite Indian models—perhaps Geronimo Gomez (known also as Star Road), or Jim Romero. It was the artists' custom to have a favored model in those days who also served the family as general factotum. As a result of these outings, Helen Blumenschein is at home in the woods and streamland around Taos and is actively engaged in preserving and studying them.

Good health and vigor were Blumenschein's fortune for most of his long life. He played baseball on the town team into his 50s and tennis, at which he won numerous awards in Paris and the United States, well into his 70s. Bridge tournaments in California and other western states lured him into travels. While crossing the wide open spaces on his way to these tourneys, he would do small postcard-size landscapes that later served as inspiration for full-sized oils. Other trips came about because he was a popular and erudite judge of competitive art exhibitions. He savored these experiences to the fullest.

For 25 years, Blumy was a member of the esteemed Salmagundi Club of New York. During World War I the club appointed him their official western representative to help in their war effort. With typical fervor he organized the Taos artists to paint range-finder landscapes used by the artillery in gunnery training.

Competition was sweet to Blumenschein. His drive was to reach perfection and artistic success, not for money but for recognition. The awards he won and the honors accrued to him are of such a high order, so widely distributed nationally and internationally, and spread over so many years that it is impractical to list them all. But a few will indicate the quality of recognition he was granted.

Ernest L. Blumenschein was elected an Associate of the National Academy of Design in 1912 and to full membership in 1927. In 1916 he won a most appropriate commission to interpret the American composer Edward Alexander MacDowell's piano piece "Indian Suite" in a painting for the Steinway Collection. He titled it *Flight of Arrows.* The Chicago Art Institute awarded him the Potter Palmer Gold Medal in 1917, and with it $1000. Large monetary awards accounted for a vital part of his income in the early years. His painting *Superstition*, now owned by the Gilcrease Institute, won the Altman prize of $1000 in 1921 at the National Academy of Design. He took the Logan Prize at the Academy twice, in 1929 and again in 1931. Prizes and good reviews continued to come his way. In his later years the University of New Mexico awarded him an Honorary Master of Art degree in 1927. In 1948 the Museum of New Mexico held a retrospective of 65 paintings, the first such show ever held at the museum.

Taos Creek. *Oil, 25 x 30″ (64 x 76 cm). Fenn Galleries, Ltd., Santa Fe.*

IN HIS LATER YEARS it was difficult for Blumy to finish a painting. He painted, repainted, and returned to paint again. This habit is partially responsible for the density of his pigment. The heavily ridged pattern of strokes makes an identifiably Blumenschein surface. Not only did the artist rework pictures after they had been exhibited, but he also destroyed many. Bickerstaff reported that he burned 150 paintings before leaving New York. Later he had two more fires of other work. Quite possibly he burned work the world would have considered excellent, for Blumenschein painted some true masterpieces. He is said to have regretted the destruction of some paintings long afterward.

An unforgettable painting now owned by the Museum of Modern Art, is his *Jury for Trial of a Sheepherder* (above). In his own estimation, this was Blumenschein's finest work. It was widely exhibited in the United States and France.

The painting, a group portrait of a dozen Spanish men sitting below a balcony built in southwest adobe style, tells us far more than it at first seems to do. The dolorous sympathy, coupled with stern judgment, on the faces of these weathered men closely bound in the jury box suggest the identification and isolation of the men as a cultural unit. With irony, the artist included a faint portrait of George Washington hanging above the men, emphasizing the alien laws to which they were submitting.

In a search for models Blumenschein would walk around the plaza scrutinizing faces, and then go back to his studio and sketch them from memory. He had witnessed a similar trial the year before he painted the work *Jury for Trial of a Sheepherder*, and it affected him emotionally. His empathy, so often buried under sardonic wit in face-to-face confrontations, has welled up in this work. And the situation is as true today as it was then.

Another of his best paintings, also interestingly enough of a Spanish subject, is *The Plasterer* (page 56). In their first years at Taos, at the eastern end of the house, the Blumenscheins had a neighbor, Epimenio Tenorio, a member of the Penitente sect. Helen can recall hearing him practice his mournful songs because his voice could be heard right through the wall into what was her bedroom. Tenorio modeled for this portrait, sitting with his tools on the hearth of the Spanish-style fireplace he had built. The honesty of presentation, the skillful modeling under a bright side light, and the details of a sandstone head on the mantel and floor, all remind one of Manet, who also found inspiration from Spanish models. In the very simplicity of *The Plasterer* there is a timeless dignity, so well captured by the artist that he could ask little more of himself.

In the early '20s the State of Missouri commissioned a group of Taos artists to paint murals for the new capitol building in Jefferson City. Blumenschein painted three historical lunettes and two single, full-length portraits, one of General John J. Pershing, who posed for the work, and one of George Caleb Bingham, the frontier artist. To paint the lunettes, Blumenschein had to add ten feet (3m) to the north front of Epimenio Tenorio's old room which he had bought after Tenorio's death. He filled the upper wall with a studio window. It was in this room also that he painted the jury.

When Helen Blumenschein returned from school in the East, she lived and painted in this complete studio apartment. Blumenschein had by then taken over the large central room in the house for his own studio. His wife's studio was the westernmost room. Today the home is owned by the Kit Carson Memorial Foundation. Still to be seen in the high-ceilinged room are pieces of handsome furniture originally bought in Paris by Mary Blumenschein's mother. Through the deepset windows is a distant view of the Taos Valley.

Desert Mining Camp. *Oil, 23 x 33" (58 x 84 cm). Collection the Harwood Foundation, University of New Mexico.*

URING HIS 86 YEARS, Blumenschein followed the principles of picture making he had learned as a student, but he did so thoughtfully, and he had the ability to put his credo into words. Laura Bickerstaff quotes the following admirable advice from his notes:

"First: Try to appreciate all schools of art if they have virility. Do not approach a painting with set formula in your mind as to what it should contain. The painting of the whole world has many points of view. You will obtain great satisfaction and inspiration to your own endeavors by being able to enjoy the art of all races.

"Second: Be yourself—and trust your subconscious taste—with always a desire to learn and grow.

"Third: Establish your planes with color as well as perspective.

"Fourth: Search distinguished tones.

"Fifth: Make memory sketches.

"Sixth: Ask yourself when contemplating your work: *Are your masses large? Is your design vigorous?* Are your proportions or spaces beautiful in their relations? Is the brush craftsmanship able (although this to me is of slight importance, it sometimes adds great charm)? Is your picture like many others—or have you said something that is your own? Is it decorative as well as realistic? Realistic alone is deadly commonplace."

These entwined precepts curiously reflect those academic adages taught at European academies and those schools modeled upon them, particularly the references to distinguished tones and memory sketches; however, they also are contemporary in their consciousness of self-expression and self-trust.

Blumenschein did not hide his viewpoint; he was always expressive and quotable. After a trip to San Francisco in 1953, Bickerstaff reported that he said of modern art: "We cannot burst the links of the traditional ideals of man, and with a flood of propaganda endeavor to create new ideals that lack the depth of centuries. I can appreciate skillful ingenuity. I can be highly pleased with extraordinary color or design, but I will never again compare these works that build no form, with the grandeur of thought and feeling which have been expressed in our masterpieces. . . ."

He was 79 when he wrote these words, and they are lucid despite the encroachment of arteriosclerosis of the brain, the disease that had prompted his trip to sea level because it was thought the altitude of Taos hastened the progress of the illness.

There is an evolution in Blumenschein's work. He maintained a conservative style, but he was always aware of and open to the developments of contemporary art. (By the time of his death in 1960, avant-garde work was being shown in nearby galleries.) The first major change he made in his work was to forego illustration. After 1919 he also left behind the dark palette of the àcademies in favor of one more suited to the brilliance and vast distances of the southwestern landscape. His work became increasingly decorative as he sought surface qualities for their own sake. Figures were common in his early paintings, but later became less frequent. All but a few of his so-called "Indian" paintings were sold during his lifetime, and the rest were snatched up almost immediately after his death. Unlike many artists, Blumenschein was left with just a small stock of work.

Blumenschein was the best known of the early Taos group and the most intellectual. He knew the direction art was taking after the Post-Impressionist period and derived ideas from the modern movement that strengthened his invention without lessening the impact of his imagery. His work traveled the world from New Zealand to Paris and throughout the United States carrying his sympathetic and original view of the southwestern people and landscape. He won popular and critical acclaim.

In his gouache *Self-Portrait* of 1948 (not shown here), Blumenschein painted both a stern likeness and an exercise in symbolic design. The hatchwork on the head and jacket functions as a consciously chosen pattern. The row of Indians, pueblo architectural elements and sun symbol form a lively background. Blumenschein reveals himself to be a fine observer who faithfully records his own wrinkles and white hair, but within the decorative areas he implies that the Indians' life and Taos area are the stuff of his dreams.

Regina Tatum Cooke, longtime art correspondent of the variously named Taos newspaper, remembers fellow-artist Blumenschein: "Blumy would walk down the street and everyone knew him. He was always approachable and friendly in spite of his sometimes sharp wit. Once he painted a string of boxcars and used paint remover to redo parts of his canvas. It left a gray steamy look that he liked. 'I hope I have the guts to leave it alone,' he said."

In the last decade of his life, Helen Blumenschein saw a gradual change in her father as the arteriosclerosis had its effect. For months of each year he lived in Albuquerque to get away from the higher altitude of Taos. True to his nature, he painted. His scenes of the railroad yards and rooftops of Albuquerque in simplified, bold compositions are among his final works. He won the top award in the New Mexico State Fair Juried Exhibition of 1953 with just such a painting.

OSCAR E. BERNINGHAUS
Modesty and Expertise

GENTLE MANNERS AND a generous public spirit made Oscar E. Berninghaus a welcome addition to Taos, a town he first saw after a unique sightseeing trip through the Rockies as a guest of the Denver and Rio Grande Railroad in 1899.

After serving as an apprentice, "Bernie" (as he was always known), had succeeded at his job in a commercial lithography plant in his native St. Louis and as a reward was granted a month's paid vacation. He headed first to Denver and then to Antonito, Colorado. While waiting on the platform there for the southbound train, Bernie spent his time sketching. A railroad man happened along and, fascinated by this unexpected sight, was inspired to help the young artist enjoy the scenery in special way. He told Bernie that the best view was from the roof of the train, and he then tied Bernie into a chair securely roped to the catwalk of the baggage car. In this regal, albeit risky, manner, Berninghaus arrived at the train junction of Servilletta, New Mexico and caught a buckboard to Taos. The loquacious railroader had filled his mind with glowing reports of the people and sights of Taos, and Bernie was not disappointed.

He arrived in late afternoon just as the Sangre de Cristo mountains turned pink at sunset. His description of the village as he saw it on that trip was quoted by Bickerstaff from a letter Berninghaus wrote in 1950: "... a barren plaza with hitching rail around it, covered wagons of home seekers, cow and Indian ponies hitched to it. A few merchants and too many saloons made up the business section; there were comparatively few Anglos, some of these had mining interests, some were health seekers, and some perhaps fugitives from justice, as Taos might well be a good hide-out place at the time. I found one artist, with whom I soon became acquainted. It was Bert Phillips. He came in 1898, liked it so well he hung his hat on a peg and there it has remained ever since. I stayed here but a week, became infected with the Taos germ and promised myself a longer stay the following year. . . ."

Berninghaus returned to his lithography job and stayed there a number of months more. As a result of hard work and night classes at both Washington University and the St. Louis School of Fine Arts, he had become an accomplished designer, draftsman, and printmaker, and he decided to become an independent commercial artist too. His most lucrative account was with the Anheuser-Busch Brewery for whom Berninghaus did advertisements. On the strength of this income, he married Emelia Miller in 1900. The couple had two children, a son Charles and a daughter Dorothy. Their happy marriage ended with the untimely death of his wife in 1913.

With his dutiful family-oriented nature, Berninghaus fully assumed the responsibility of raising his children. He came from a first-generation German family and was the oldest of their five children. His father was a lithograph salesman who provided well, but modestly. There were refined manners, industry, and loyalty in the home of his childhood, and Berninghaus saw to it that he gave the same background to his own children. He soon developed a seasonal rhythm that revolved around their schooling. Each winter they lived in St. Louis while Charles and Dorothy went to school; then they spent their summers in Taos, continuing a tradition he had started before his wife died.

In 1912, while the family was in Taos, Oscar E. Berninghaus joined in founding the Taos Society of Artists. Thereafter he sent his paintings on circuit shows with the society. Sales became more frequent and Berninghaus would supply a replacement for any work sold during the tour, just as the others of the group did.

In St. Louis, Berninghaus became a successful artist. There he was well known for helping on city booster projects, and each year he designed floats for the St. Louis Veiled Prophet Pageant. But his creative paintings also did well in competitive exhibitions. In 1915 he won the Mary Elizabeth Bascom prize for figure painting in the second annual competition of the Artists Guild with his *Taos Pueblo Indian, New Mexico*. At the National Academy of Design he won the Ranger Fund Prize in 1925 with *Their Son* and the Altman Prize in 1926 with *A Hunter of Taos*.

Photo Laura Gilpin

Truchas Peaks from the Mesa. *Oil, 20 x 24″ (51 x 61 cm). McAdoo Galleries, Inc., Woodrow Wilson Fine Arts.*

Forgotten. *Oil, 24 x 30" (61 x 76 cm). Fenn Galleries Ltd., Santa Fe.*

Little Joe in the Studio. *Oil, 36 x 32" (91 x 81 cm).*
Collection Museum of Fine Arts, Museum of New Mexico, Santa Fe.

On the Mesa. *Oil, 20 x 24" (51 x 61 cm). McAdoo Galleries, Inc., Woodrow Wilson Fine Arts.*

BERNINGHAUS BOUGHT his home in Taos in 1919 but he continued his dual residence and dual career until 1925. At that time he moved permanently to his lovely rambling adobe home on the *Loma*, that is, up on the hill. In the front yard was an old well, and next to the house was his new Model-T Ford, a sign of affluence and a necessary aid to him on his sketching jaunts to the mountains.

Berninghaus excelled at drawing horses in the southwestern landscape. He also painted Indian studies and western men in their outdoor settings. Among his favorite models were three Taos Indians: Albert Martinez (Looking Elk), Tony Lujan, and Little Joe Gomez (see page 36). Each of them at different times sat for hours as models, served in the home as domestic help, and accompanied the artist on his camping-sketching trips.

Through the '20s Berninghaus received favorable reviews that compared his work to that of Remington and Russell. During those years he was commissioned to paint five lunettes for the new capitol of Missouri at Jefferson City. Undoubtedly the commission was welcome to Berninghaus as a financial help, but others were never aware that there was any economic strain on him, for the artist had a quality that permeated all his dealings—an orderly, precise control over his affairs. Bills were always paid, records were always kept, and duties were always done, though no one remembers him as a fussy or stodgy person.

The friendship between Berninghaus and Bert Phillips lasted throughout their lives. In a letter written to Phillips in 1902, Berninghaus reveals his innate modesty: "I have been asked to contribute a picture to the exhibitions—and what do you think—*it passed the jury* so that is the first time any picture was rated among the artists whom I have considered so far above me. You know I am only a common commercial artist accustomed to drawing tables, buildings, tomato cans, labels, etc."

Seventy-four years after this was written, Mr. and Mrs. August A. Busch donated some 50 works by Oscar E. Berninghaus, done for the Anheuser-Busch Brewery, to the St. Louis Art Museum. "The Berninghaus collection is valued by Busch at approximately $1 million," John Brod Peters reported in the *Globe-Democrat*. Through all those years, the work Berninghaus felt was "common commercialism" was displayed by the Busch family at their estate and at the brewery.

Another quality, that of generous concern for others, was revealed in Berninghaus' letter, when he wrote to Phillips: "Sometime when you get a little sketch that don't amount to much, to you, and you want to sell cheap, I should like to take it off you for my home—I have quite a few of various artists, and I should like ever so much to have you represented."

Berninghaus never studied abroad nor indulged his talent in self-centered ways. Even as a youth he always had obligations to others, but he had honed his talent, learning the market and necessities of a career. In 1926 he was elected an Associate of the National Academy, but he never completed the required steps to become a full member, although he did paint a self-portrait in 1951. (It is now at the Gilcrease Institute of Art in Tulsa, Oklahoma—the Gilcrease owns a major collection of his work. Other collections are owned by the Museum of New Mexico, Santa Fe; the Anschutz Collection, Denver; the Harrison Eiteljorg Collection, Indianapolis; and the Cowboy Hall of Fame, Oklahoma City.)

In this self-portrait, Berninghaus showed himself frankly as a slightly built, unaggressive man in glasses with short hair and a white shirt. He wore gold-rimmed glasses and, at 77, was energetic-looking and bright-eyed.

The order and neatness of his person and of his habits were also characteristic of his paintings. Berninghaus created logical paintings whose spaces were clearly defined as foreground, middleground, and distance. The scale he favored was one that placed man or animal in nature but not in a dominating position. There was a balance between his focus on the setting and on the action. Bickerstaff has noted that in his later paintings he withdrew to a more distant viewpoint so that the scene was wider and the figures smaller.

In the Petrified Forest. *Oil, 25 x 30" (64 x 76 cm). Fenn Galleries Ltd., Santa Fe.*

Taos Scene. *Oil, 12 x 16" (31 x 41 cm). Fenn Galleries Ltd., Santa Fe.*

Martinez Hacienda. *Oil, 20 x 24" (51 x 61 cm). Private collection.*

T AOS AND ITS ENVIRONMENT are strongly sunlit, and different artists have reflected this in varied ways. Some stressed the brightness of the light, but Berninghaus captured another quality of light that is also often seen in Taos, a softened brightness that gives a pastel tone to the landscape.

Another Berninghaus touch is a flickering stroke of short length, one that is controlled and evenly distributed, that gives a particular texture to his surfaces. The way he drew and painted with his brush was pleasingly "right" and accurate. He would look upon a scene and find it paintable, then bring his considerable talent to bear on recreating it. He especially favored the Ranchitos Valley below his home, and landscapes of fall and spring as the trees changed color.

For years Berninghaus painted models from life and landscapes from nature. In later years, however, his repertoire of stored images was so large that he was able to paint from memory as accurately as he used to from sketching.

There is an undercurrent in Berninghaus' work that is far more philosophical than one might suspect at first glance; his objectivity camouflaged a sensitive appraisal of his Indian neighbors. Van Deren Coke describes this quiet profundity in *Taos and Santa Fe/The Artists' Environment*: "Unlike some of his associates in Taos, Berninghaus' sophisticated early illustrative style was used as a frame to hold his spectators' attention, while he slowly unfolded his observations of the inner truth surrounding the life of a twentieth-century Taos Indian."

Berninghaus filled a special role in Taos as a respected, genuinely liked man. For almost 20 years he was a widower who entertained graciously, enjoyed card games, conviviality, and good food. He seemed at peace with himself as an artist and as a father. In 1932, 19 years after the death of his first wife, Berninghaus married Winnifred Shuler from Raton. They had a happy 20 years together. Though they traveled at first, in the last years of his life, Bernie never left Taos. He died there on April 27, 1952, at 78.

J. Charles Berninghaus, who continues in his father's tradition as a landscapist of note, still lives in Taos. So does Dorothy Berninghaus Brandenburg, now the wife of a banker, who serves on numerous commissions and carries on the family tradition of public service. Winnifred Berninghaus died in 1969.

Oscar E. Berninghaus had a wide reputation and a worldly understanding of just how art history is made. He knew quite well that he and his Taos colleagues filled a historic niche. Bickerstaff quotes a newspaper interview he gave in 1927: "I think the colony in Taos is doing much for American art. From it I think will come a distinctive art, something definitely American—and I do not mean that such will be the case because the American Indian and his environment are the subjects. But the canvases that come from Taos are as definitely American as anything can be. We have had French, Dutch, Italian, German art. Now we must have American art. I feel that from Taos will come that art."

As usual with Berninghaus, his calm judgment and sober opinion proved to be sound.

Winter in the Panhandle. Oil, 30 x 34¼" (76 x 87 cm). The San Antonio Art League.

EANGER IRVING COUSE
The Indian as Noble Innocent

EANGER IRVING COUSE made his first trip to Taos in 1902 with his wife Virginia and his son Kibbey, aged eight. Kibbey Couse has written about that trip: "It was necessary to come down from Denver to Alamosa on the D & RG Railroad then change to the narrow gauge "Chili Line" to Tres Piedras. The "down" train reached there at 4 PM, on the rare occasions when it was on time.

"This was too late to start the long stage trip to Taos, so the Couse family put up at the only hotel . . . at the head of the Hondo Canyon. This hostelry had the rooms partitioned off by two by fours at the eight foot level to which cheese-cloth walls were tacked. Hardly soundproof! And the rats had a Roman holiday racing along the network of two by fours. Mrs. Couse took this in her stride. She was a true western girl who had spent her childhood on the Walker ranch.

"The next day dawned with a June blizzard. It cleared about noon and the stage started out, but got no farther than the half-way house on the Rio Grande River at John Dunn's bridge . . . built and operated by the stage line proprietor, the famous Long John Dunn.

"The next morning the snow had mostly evaporated . . . and we had no trouble reaching Taos before noon. Bert Phillips met us with his wife Rose. They had a house next to their own residence already rented for us from Filipe Gutman. There and then the Couse-Phillips lifelong friendship began its even course."

Taos wrought its magical attraction on Couse and he arranged his life to spend as many months as possible in Taos each year until 1927, when he became a permanent resident.

"Irv" Couse was born in Saginaw, Michigan, on September 3, 1866, and grew up in that remote logging center, home of the Chippewa and Ojibwa Indians. They were the earliest subjects on which he exerted an innate talent for drawing. The art he knew best was the work of Indian painters. Classic painting was unknown to him, yet he planned to become an artist and he worked as a housepainter for funds to study art. In 1884, at the age of 18, he was able to spend three months at the Chicago Art Institute before his money ran out. Undaunted, he returned home for another season of housepainting.

For the next two years, 1885-1887, Couse was a student at the National Academy of Design in New York. He cared intensely about his studies and did odd jobs to earn his way. Each year he won awards at the academy's student exhibitions: the silver medal for the antique class (drawing from plaster models) in 1885 and the bronze medal in the life class in 1886.

On returning to Saginaw, Couse painted portraits of his townsmen for a year and then went to Paris in 1887 where he studied under Robert Fleury and Adolphe Bouguereau at the Académie Julien. Bouguereau was the consummate academician whose style was extremely popular. Couse, a talented pupil, followed the academic tradition enthusiastically. For four years he won awards at the academy, which confirmed his skill and taste.

In 1891, while in Paris, he married fellow art student Virginia Walker, a rancher's daughter from Washington near the Oregon border. After their marriage they traveled to the ranch for a visit and Couse painted among the Klikitat, Yakima, and Umatilla tribes in the vicinity. These small, rosy-sky scenes are charmingly deft, with painterly brushwork. Slightly more sketchy than in his later work, their deep pastel hues are reminiscent of the Barbizon school in France. In fact, there is a strong link between the vision of the Barbizon painters and that of Irving Couse. Both attempted to paint "simple folk" in a natural setting and both embued the model with heroic form.

Couse made a direct progression from drawing casts of classic statues to painting Indians as though they were classic models. His technical mastery of painting was formidable and the imprint of his French academic training never faded in Couse's work.

The entire Couse family, including son Kibbey who was born in 1894 in Etaples, a coastal village, lived in France for several years. Within Couse's work is a group of French landscapes similar to his northwest American pieces: direct, broadly painted scenes of coastal fishing and pastorals of shepherds. These also were painted in low-key pastel colors. A pale full moon can be found in several of these paintings. The emphasis was on beauty and serenity.

Couse met Joseph Henry Sharp and Ernest L. Blumenschein, who were both in Paris studying at the Academy in 1899. He told them, no doubt, about his youthful knowledge of the Chippewa and Ojibwa Indians and his more recent trip to Washington and Oregon. Sharp had also visited the area, so there was bond of mutual interest among the men from the beginning. They told Couse about the Pueblo Indians of Taos and their relative isolation and the pageantry of their ceremonial life. All this caught Couse's imagination thoroughly.

These men held a unique idea in common, that of creating an art that was American in subject. Though it did not seem necessary to them to change styles, they did feel a powerful urge to explore the Indian subject as something removed from the domination of the Academy. To them, art was a discipline whose dictates were well established by history and whose demands for constant study and practice they accepted without reluctance. But they were not satisfied to apply their skills to a series of still lifes, nudes, or salon portraits. They sought fresh material. This desire for the unexplored formed the basis of their conviviality.

Chief Shappanagons. *Oil, 19 x 9" (48 x 23 cm). McAdoo Galleries, Inc.,*
Woodrow Wilson Fine Arts, Santa Fe.

ON RETURNING to the States, Couse established his studio in New York and traveled once again to the Northwest, but in 1902 he made the trip to Taos so well described by Kibbey Couse. The year 1902 was a landmark in the Couse career. Not only did he find his permanent reference and home in Taos, but he also became an Associate of the National Academy of Design and won the First Hallgarten Prize for his painting *Peace Pipe*, painted in Oregon.

For a few years Couse earned his living from portraits, but he was a shrewd businessman and he understood the need to market his work from a New York base. By maintaining a studio in the city and always being present during the winter exhibition season, he created the network of contacts artists must have in order to sell their work.

Although the modern movement in art began in France and was transported to the United States at the turn of the century and thereafter, the taste of the public was more aroused by visions of the vanishing West. The romance of unseen, but still American, Indians in their own setting was as desirable to the art buyers as it was heartwarming to Irving Couse.

This was also a period of expansion for America's railroads. From 1922 to 1934, paintings by Irving Couse were on the calendars distributed by the Santa Fe Railway as part of their concerted publicity campaign to attract passengers to the Southwest. The original oils became a part of the impressive collection owned by the railroad, and prints of them were hung in waiting rooms across the country. Even after his death, Couse's work was featured on the calendar three times, in 1937, 1938, and 1962.

More than any other early Taos artist, Couse, with his loving faith in the Indian, spoke directly to the sensitivities of his time. After the Federal government pursued a ruthless conquest of the Indians based on a view of them as savage and therefore expendable, the Indian nation was vanquished, and only vestiges of the tribes remained. But by then, the frontier was also gone and people felt differently about the Indian race. With a more humane federal policy of paternal concern in its infancy, and in the midst of a developing nationalism, the nation was ready for Couse's image of a tranquil, unthreatening, beautiful American Indian.

Contemporary critical evaluations of Couse's work show a wide latitude. In 1963 Van Deren Coke wrote: "Couse had an obvious sympathy for his subjects and although he may have been the victim of a taste for sentimental idealism, there is, nevertheless, a sincerity and technical proficiency which must be admired as artifice of a high order."

Harold McCracken wrote in an essay for Fenn Galleries, Ltd., Santa Fe, for their large show of Couse's work in 1974: "Eanger Irving Couse as an artist can probably best be described as a poet with paint brushes rather than pencils or a typewriter. . . . The Indian paintings Couse put on canvas have the distinctiveness which is the hallmark of a great artist. It does not take any great amount of expertise to recognize a Couse picture, even at a considerable distance and without looking at the signature." The latter remark is accurate in that Couse's paintings are consistent in style, technique, and even further, the figure itself becomes familiar after seeing a number of his pictures.

Couse used only a few models; mostly he painted John Concha and Ben Lujan, who first posed for him at the age of 12. Day after day in later years Ben Lujan would arrive at Couse's door about 8:30 in the morning. Lujan was primarily a model, but he was also a handyman and always a warm friend of the Couse family. By 9:00 Couse would begin painting. He painted only by the strong morning light in his ample studio.

nch Model. Oil, 20 x 16" (51 x 41 cm). McAdoo Galleries, Inc., Woodrow Wilson Fine Arts, Santa Fe.

Moki Snake Dance. *Oil, 36 x 48" (91 x 122 cm). The Anschutz Collection, Denver.*

THE COUSE HOME, which was next door to the Sharp home, was a former convent and it still retained its chapel, walled forecourt, and bell. When Couse bought it in 1910, it had dirt floors and a flat roof, but he later laid down wooden floors. His son Kibbey, who was 15 years old then, remembers his father complaining of an aching back from the unusually strenuous task. Couse was a comfortably built, rotund man, not much given to such intense physical work.

The flat studio roof was also removed and a sloping one with a great north window was built. A wall was also removed to make a bigger area for the studio. In one corner, a fine Taos-style curved fireplace with a mantel and hearth was built. Around the ceiling and in likely spots throughout the studio, Couse displayed his magnificent collection of Indian pottery from New Mexico and Arizona, collected on painting trips and visits to ceremonies. Some of the pots were tokens of "give-away dances" at which guests were encouraged to take the pottery offered. Ben Lujan often posed beside the fireplace with one of these fine pots nearby.

Couse's work contains certain recognizable characteristics: a sparsely clad Indian crouches in profile or squats on his heels; he is lit by firelight, strong sidelight, or moonlight that dramatizes his muscular form; he is engaged in a domestic act, such as drum-making, bead-drilling, wall painting, or praying; he has a pensive withdrawn expression and is sealed in privacy. Details of gear are used for pictorial effect rather than strict accuracy. Couse was always the painter, not the reporter. Yet he was so involved with the Taos people that he conveyed a feeling of contact with their sacred rituals. For them, daily tasks, however repetitive, are made significant and dignified by their association with prayer, in the form of a song or an action. Couse sensitively added an appropriate tone of reverence to his paintings, even though he usually composed and painted them in his studio.

There was one major exception to Couse's preferred approach to paintings, and this was *Moki Snake Dance* (page 46), where he accurately portrayed the Hopi ceremony. He and his family had traveled to Walpi, Arizona, in 1903 and had watched the annual summer festival which lasted for six weeks. Couse was moved to paint this work, perhaps his greatest painting, in a classic manner. He captures the mystery and pageantry with a Renaissance-like feeling of monumentality. Couse saw the ritual as the heart of the Hopi religion, just as a Renaissance painter stressed the importance, for example, of a majestic Nativity.

Couse was apparently a slow, methodical painter, but he was also a steady one, and over his fairly long career he created over 1500 oils. Some are now in the Metropolitan Museum of Art, the National Gallery of the Smithsonian Institution, the Dallas Museum of Fine Art, the Detroit Institute of Art, the Milwaukee Art Center, the Toledo Museum of Art, the Philbrook Art Center and Gilcrease Institute of Art (both in Tulsa), and the Museum of New Mexico, among numerous other collections. In 1911 Couse was elected to full membership in the National Academy.

Couse once said he believed in hard work, not inspiration, but he frequently sketched outdoors in the canyons or up among the aspens on the Taos mountains, and would take his Indian model with him on these excursions. However, his finished work was painted in his studio, where there were several large easels, and Couse often had more than one painting in progress at a time. He also had a large draped model stand placed to allow the northern light to shower down upon it.

French Peasant Girl, *1890. Oil, 16 x 13" (41 x 33 cm).*
Mr. and Mrs. Woodrow Wilson.

AROUND 1900, a friend sent Couse planks of mahogany from Central America, and he built his own paint table with them. The neatly hinged cabinet with four drawers is still filled with his paints and remains in his studio. In the early years, Couse only sketched in New Mexico and did his paintings in New York. But eventually he brought everything to Taos, where it still remains today.

Surrounding the Couse home was one of the finest and most beautiful of Taos gardens. The *L*-shaped house with its portal shelters the garden just at the edge of an arroyo. Even now, the beauty it once had can still be appreciated. Virginia Walker Couse gave up her own career as a painter and turned to this garden for aesthetic satisfaction. Ben Lujan became the family gardener and assisted her in the project, working in the afternoons after his posing was over for the day.

Couse collected things such as Spanish *santos* and *retablos* (painted wood figures and pictures of saints). He bought some of these *santos*, now rare and expensive, for only a dollar apiece. They were displayed on fireplaces around his home.

When Couse decided to bring water to his house, he found he could not dig near the chapel because there was a burial ground underneath it. So he ran pipes high up under the ceilings, thus adapting the house to his needs without violating the history of the place.

People remember Couse as a man of equilibrium and amicability. He was handsome in a country-gentleman sort of way, with an aristocratic nose and a trim little beard and mustache. There was more than a hint of his Alsatian forebears in his face.

The Taos Indians liked Couse and called him Green Mountain; they were referring both to his ample size and to his preference for a worn old pair of cords and a green sweater. Indian friends attended his funeral and then stayed behind to offer up their own prayer for Green Mountain.

When Couse served as president of the Taos Society of Artists, his vigorous sense of the marketplace was especially useful. He was a loyal and helpful friend. A 1902 letter to Bert Phillips shows that he did errands for Phillips while in New York, nitty-gritty things like ordering his frames and reporting on where Phillips' painting would hang at an exhibition.

In his later years he was remembered as a man who greatly enjoyed the movies. He attended almost every film, despite the banter of other movie addicts such as Blumenschein and Ufer.

In 1929 Virginia Couse died and her loss took its toll on Couse. He continued painting, but some say he lost his spark. He died in 1936 in Taos, leaving his faithful companion Ben Lujan bereft. Until his death several years ago, Ben Lujan was known in Taos as Ben Couse.

His son Kibbey Couse, a successful engineer and inventor, resided in the house in the summers until his death in 1978. For over 40 years Kibbey generously maintained his father's studio intact for the benefit of interested visitors.

Indian Irrigating His Corn. *Oil, 36″ x 24″ (91 x 61 cm). Private collection.*

Sharp's Studio. Oil, 20 x 30' (51 x 76 cm). Fenn Galleries Ltd., Santa Fe.

Gladiolas. *Oil, 24 x 20' (61 x 51 cm).*
McAdoo Galleries, Inc., Woodrow Wilson Fine Arts.

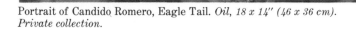

Portrait of Candido Romero, Eagle Tail. *Oil, 18 x 14' (46 x 36 cm).*
Private collection.

Joseph Henry Sharp

Taos Pueblo, 1918. *Oil, 36 x 48″ (91 x 122 cm). Fenn Galleries Ltd., Santa Fe.*

Francisco Martini. *Oil, 41 x 48″ (104 x 122 cm). Collection Harrison Eiteljorg.*

ne Santero. *Oil, 30 x 25'' (76 x 64 cm). The Anschutz Collection.*

My Patio. *Oil, 14 x 18″ (36 x 46 cm). Private collection.*

Deer Hunting Camp. *Oil, 24 x 36" (61 x 91 cm). Collection Harrison Eiteljorg.*

Taos Indian. *Oil, 19 x 15" (48 x 38 cm). The Santa Fe Collection of Southwestern Art.*

The Secret Olla. *Oil, 25 x 29" (64 x 74 cm). The Santa Fe Collection of Southwestern Art.*

The Plasterer. *Oil, 42 x 30" (107 x 76 cm). Collection Harrison Eiteljorg.*

Penitentes. *Oil, 23 x 50'' (58 x 127 cm). Collection Harrison Eiteljorg.*

The Peacemaker, *1913. Oil, 50 x 50'' (127 x 102 cm). The Anschutz Collection.*

Ernest L. Blumenschein

Taos Indian with Jug. *Oil, 30 x 25″ (76 x 64 cm). The Santa Fe Collection of Southwestern Art.*

Rio Grande Gorge Near Taos. *Oil, 27 x 48″ (69 x 122 cm). Eugene B. Adkins Collection.*

Moving Day. *Oil, 30 x 40" (76 x 102 cm). Courtesy Harrison Eiteljorg.*

Ricardo and His Horses. *Oil, 16 x 20" (41 x 51 cm). Eugene B. Adkins Collection.*

Oscar E. Berninghaus

Autumn in Indian Country. *Oil, 35 x 40" (89 x 102 cm). Fenn Galleries Ltd., Santa Fe.*

Cotton Picking. *30¼ x 34¼" (77 x 87 cm). The San Antonio Art League.*

The Wedding. *Oil, 70 x 37″ (178 x 94 cm). Collection Harrison Eiteljorg.*

Eanger Irving Couse

Elk Foot, 1911. Oil, 32½ x 16" (82 x 41 cm). Collection Museum of Fine Arts, Museum of New Mexico, Santa Fe.

The Archery Lesson. Oil, 24 x 29" (61 x 74 cm). Fenn Galleries Ltd., Santa Fe.

The Drummer. Oil, 36 x 46" (91 x 117 cm). Fenn Galleries, Ltd., Santa Fe.

Flute Players by Moonlight.
Oil, 30 x 36" (76 x 91 cm).
Fenn Galleries Ltd., Santa Fe.

The Conjurer. *Oil, 35¼ x 46¼" (90 x 117 cm). Fenn Galleries, Ltd., Santa Fe.*

WILLIAM HERBERT DUNTON
From Yankee to Cowboy

The Old Santa Fe Trail. *Oil, 26 x 32" (66 x 81 cm). The Santa Fe Collection of Southwestern Art.*

WILLIAM HERBERT DUNTON was one of America's top-ranking illustrators, but he abandoned this career and moved to Taos in 1912. Soon after he arrived, six men formed the famous Taos Society of Artists, and 'Buck' Dunton was one of them.

A transplanted Yankee, Dunton was born August 28, 1878, in Augusta, Maine, where he grew up in rural comfort on family farms. Among his boyhood pleasures were fishing and hunting in the Maine woods with his brother and grandfather. He remained an outdoorsman all his life.

Apparently Dunton hated school, but he loved to draw. His family appreciated his talent and fostered it by providing him with neatly bound sketchbooks. IIe took these sketchbooks everywhere on his treks, avidly recording in them details of nature. Animals fascinated him even then.

Others admired his work too, among them the editors of the Boston *Globe* and the Lewiston and Bangor newspapers, who began buying the enterprising boy's sketches. At 16 he quit school, took a job, and continued to sell sketches to the papers.

Two years later he made a lengthy trip to Montana, following his boyish dream of freedom in the West. With him he took his sketchbook and paints with the intention of studying large game. Laura Bickerstaff believes Dunton began his analytical, step-by-step approach to animal anatomy during this early trip. His method thoroughly combined his interest in hunting with that of art.

In drawing a mountain lion, for example, he would begin by repeatedly sketching the live animal. He then would shoot the animal and possibly freeze it, depending on weather conditions. In detailed sketches he would record the head, paws, and fur, taking his time to study different lighting effects. As he systematically dissected the creature, he sketched the musculature and, eventually, the skeleton. Schools may have confined him unduly, but scholarly solitary study did not. Once he developed his study system, he kept it up for years and continued to expand his knowledge of the animal kingdom.

For the next 15 years he returned to the West regularly and hired himself out to work on cattle ranches. His travels took him from Oregon into Mexico where he had to run for his life during the Madero revolution against Diaz. Dunton became a full-fledged cowboy, but only a part-time one; he always returned to New York, where he applied himself to his well-earned commissions for commercial illustrations.

His long hours in the saddle gave him a chance to sketch and paint; his materials were always right in his saddlebags. By living with cowboys, working beside them, and painting them on location, Dunton became an expert illustrator of outdoor western life. As his career widened, he did paintings of sports themes and romance for the best men's and women's magazines. He also illustrated 49 books, the best known of which are *Riders of the Purple Sage, Wanderer of the Wasteland,* and *Under Western Stars* by Zane Grey. Dunton was a published writer himself, with a flair for description. He continued to write through the years and occasionally illustrated his own stories. It was a habit of his to describe his paintings and their meaning either in letters or articles, thus making his own record of his art.

Success quickly came to him in his early 20s. At 21 he married Nellie Hartley, but he often found his art conflicted with his role as husband-father. It must have been a difficult life for the young couple; they were often separated for months at a time while Buck Dunton was out West. Then, on returning to New York, he would flail himself with work. The volume of his production was enormous and his economic success reflected it. As his reputation grew, more and more commissions came his way.

Dunton was a member of the exclusive artists social club, the Salmagundi in New York. It was there that he met Ernest L. Blumenschein in 1911. At that time Blumenschein was also a well-known, successful illustrator, slightly older than Dunton, who wintered in New York and spent every summer in Taos.

The men enjoyed many discussions. Soon after they met, Dunton enrolled in Blumenschein's class at the Art Students League. This was not a new venture for Dunton; he had also studied there under Frank DuMond and others and earlier he had attended the Cowles School in Boston. Vicariously, Dunton had acquired an academic European approach to painting, taught him by those who had studied abroad. He was a sound painter and had an excellent command of composition.

Blumenschein developed a liking for his pupil and encouraged him to go West as he regaled him with stories of Taos and the art colony growing there around Bert Phillips, the all-year anchorman of the group. This kind of talk appealed to Dunton because he was searching for a way to change his life. He chafed under an increasing restlessness.

WHEN DUNTON FOLLOWED Blumenschein's suggestion to go to Taos in 1912, he went to stay. Now there were two permanent residents among the artists of Taos: Phillips and Dunton.

Buck Dunton became a familiar figure on the village streets. Tall and lanky, he was dressed strictly as a cowboy. There was the Stetson hat (the Stetson Company sent him a new one every year with his name gold-stamped on the sweatband), a scarf tied around the neck, long narrow trousers, and boots. There is every reason to believe Dunton loved the slow easy ways of Taos, but he brought a Yankee pace with him. He is remembered as a person who never sauntered. He always dashed along the streets to the Taos Post Office where everyone met socially then (and still does). There was an urgency in him to catch a quality of western life that was passing. Protective game laws already prevented him from further big-game hunting. The romantic untamed West was quickly coming under domination.

In the fine 1974 catalog from the Denver Art Museum, *Picturesque Images From Taos and Santa Fe*, Dunton's quote, originally in an article by F. Warner Robinson in the *American Magazine of Art* (October, 1925) was especially apt: "The West has passed—more's the pity. In another 25 years the old-time Westener will have gone, too—gone with the buffalo and the antelope. I'm going to hand down to posterity a bit of the unadulterated *real thing.*"

Buck Dunton believed in his destiny as an artist and was inspired by his belief to give up working for others and to rely on his own creativity. He painted some notable paintings, among them his full-length portrait of Nathan Dolan, called *Ginger.* This is a painting of the cowboy, par excellence. It could almost be a self-portrait because Ginger wears the same outfit Dunton himself favored. The red-haired, seasoned cowboy stands casually before a landscape, lighted by slanting sunrays, assured in his own space. It was donated to the Harwood Foundation in Taos by Dunton's family.

Rustler's Pay. *Black and white oil, 26 x 38" (66 x 97 cm). Collection Mr. and Mrs. Gerald P. Peters.*

ONE OF DUNTON'S finest paintings, *My Children* (owned by the Museum of New Mexico in Santa Fe), is evidence of his independent style (page 23). It's a 50″ x 60″ (127 x 152 cm) outdoor scene. In the clumps of chamisa in the foreground, his young son Ivan looks down at something unseen by the viewer. He is visible from the waist up; in his hands are the reins to his horse who patiently waits behind him, staring in the same direction. Vivian, his older sister, is mounted on her dark horse; she turns back to follow her brother's gaze. The eyes and placement of the figures form a V-shaped triangular base to the composition.

Ivan H. Dunton, son of the artist, writes of this painting: "The picture *My Children* was painted in the early dawn hours as the sun was rising which necessitated the rather unwilling children to arise very early to pose for the limited time that the light was just so."

The slanted sunrays illuminate the foreground; behind is a rising landscape in middle-value darks, leading to a distant storm. Dunton has executed the painting in a strong weave of side-by-side strokes whose ridges make a pattern, accentuating the modeling much as hatching does in an ink drawing. It is an effective style and one characteristic of his later work. In this painting, the strokes bring out the knit of Ivan's sweater, the prickly texture of the chamisa, and the powerful rump of Vivian's horse in a consistent but understated way. The painting is dramatically staged and the composition is locked together with the distinctive point of view Dunton often mastered.

This painting was done in the early '20s in Taos, some ten years after the Duntons moved there. It is definitely the private work of a creative artist, yet there is a hint left of a story quality that grips the viewer, making one curious about the event he has recorded.

"We, as children, spent every summer with our Dad in Taos, and a more beautiful childhood one could not ask for," writes Ivan Dunton. "We were very poor but had our horses, guns, fishing gear, etc. Our Dad took us on fishing trips, horseback many times, and often we would not see anyone else for days on end. We loved the primitive life in Taos.

"My Dad resented the encroachment of 'progress' and only conceded to the convenience of electricity for one purpose: to power his fine record player, as he loved fine music. Well water, wood-burning stoves, and outhouses were a way of life."

The Duntons' home, La Solana (The Sunny Place) is a handsome two-story adobe in central Taos facing a tiny plaza named La Loma ("the hill" in Spanish). There is a gate with a bell under its archway and a stout wall around the home. It is a solid, desirable house with a stupendous view out back to the west.

Money in Taos went far then and Dunton had earned a sizable fortune before going to the West. A mere $200 a month was enough, people say, to pay for a house, food, and general expenses for an artist and a small family. Slightly more paid for servants, a comfortable home, and some niceties. By stringent economy Dunton was able to provide a good life for his family, to go his own way, and cleave his career in two. After moving to Taos he accepted only a few commercial commissions.

Nonetheless, in the 20s he too was glad to be included in the Jefferson City, Missouri, mural project that was offered to the Taos Society of Artists. They were each to paint murals for the new state capitol there. Buck Dunton did three lunettes, painting them in Taos and shipping them to Missouri for installation. His well-researched works were: *The Pony Express Leaving St. Joseph in 1861*; *First Train Arriving at Tipton in 1858*; and *Emigrants Leaving Westport Over the Santa Fe Trail*. Dunton had an especially accurate knowledge of the necessary details he included in these paintings because he was an avid collector of gear—the armament and incidental relics of the westward march of pioneers, soldiers, and cowboys. His collection, which was extensive and complete, now belongs to the museum of his native Augusta, Maine.

Whooping It Up. Oil, 20 x 30" (51 x 76 cm). McAdoo Galleries, Inc., Woodrow Wilson Fine Arts, Santa Fe.

DURING THE DEPRESSION, Dunton turned to lithography. Among his contemporaries in Taos, Dunton was singular in his choice of subject matter, for he rarely focused on the romance of the Indian. His prints, like his paintings, were of subjects he favored, particularly animals and cowboys, although he did some portrait studies of Indians as well. His lithographs were popular and showed his skill as a draftsman to advantage. Handling the lithographic crayon in a manner similar to charcoal, he shaded in a range of subtle grays. The quarter-sheet size of most of the prints did not allow him to work in large scale, but he managed by placement and viewpoint to enhance his drawings with just a slight suggestion of setting. On the white border he executed an elaborate signature, "Buck Dunton," with "W. H. Dunton" printed neatly below it. Today there is a lively market for these prints and they are selling at around $250 to $500 apiece.

Lithography was Dunton's independent commercial venture done on his own terms. At any time he could have returned full-time to the lucrative career he had abandoned as an illustrator, but he did not do so because the life he had chosen satisfied him.

After moving to Taos, he lived outdoors much of the time, on extended camping trips. Had he been born earlier or had he been free to travel through Africa, chances are he would have been a big game hunter, for the lure of the wild never left him. He suffered under the encroachment of people filling up the West.

The need he felt to abandon society for the forest was not always compatible with family life. Eventually the strain was too great for Nellie Dunton, and so she and the children left Taos. The separation continued until Dunton's early death on March 18, 1936, in Taos. Afterward, Nellie Dunton returned to Taos with her children to claim the family home they had inherited. Vivian Dunton now resides in Alaska and her brother Ivan lives in Oregon.

At present, it is the critical fashion to consider Buck Dunton a painter of lively illustrations, drawn, composed, and painted with technical expertise; but his reputation as a fine artist is rising. The power of his best images, his concentration on the subject, and his graphic paint application are qualities of a strong, individualistic artist.

Dunton's work grew from his experience on the range and in the forest. The artist was a character who dramatized his days by acting out the cowboy image. Yet it was an accurate image. In today's artistic climate, he would be enjoying the same enthusiastic reception as members of the Cowboy Artists of America, who also attempt to keep in touch with the cowboy's life. For them it's an exercise in nostalgia but Buck Dunton participated in the *real thing*— and that was his crowning glory.

"Buck" Dunton with bearskin, early 20th century Taos. The Lucinda Martin Iliff Collection, Kit Carson Memorial Foundation, Taos.

VICTOR HIGGINS
Creative Explorer

Fenn Galleries Ltd., Santa Fe.

AMONG THE MEMBERS of the Taos Society of Artists, Victor Higgins led the field in creativity. Less content than the others with the dictates of academic painting, Higgins was open to the currents of change in art. His work can be divided into periods, and his biographer Dean Porter has done so in his excellent catalog published by the University of Notre Dame in 1975.

Victor Higgins was born into a large farm family of Irish extraction in Shelbyville, Indiana, on June 28, 1884. His first contact with paint and brush occurred when he was nine, when an itinerant, enthusiastic artist stopped to paint an advertisement on the side of the Higgins' barn. Over the several days he spent on the job, the artist introduced the boy to the wonders of paint and filled his head with "art talk" about the Chicago Art Institute and about beauty.

Farming did not interest Higgins. As he grew, he retained his vision of becoming an artist and began to paint pictures on the inside walls of his father's barn. Of the nine Higgins children, Victor was the only one with this intense drive to study art. When he was 15, his parents gave him a ticket to Indianapolis, thinking he could begin his studies there. But Higgins, who had saved some money, exchanged it for one to Chicago, a fact he ruefully admitted when he boarded the train.

For the next 11 years, Higgins remained in Chicago, studying and later teaching at the Art Institute of Chicago and the Chicago Academy of Fine Arts. In 1910 he went to Europe to continue his studies for four years in the approved fashion both in Paris, where he studied at the Académie de la Grande Chaumière under René Menard and Lucien Simon, and also in Munich under Hans Von Heyck. When he returned, his style was urbane, perhaps a bit monotonous in color, but his touch was sure in pastoral landscapes and museum copies. These were the attributes of the academic professional artist of that era.

In Europe, Higgins did not seek out the experimental leaders of Parisian art circles, and he seemed to miss entirely the Post-Impressionist ferment of Cézanne's analytical composition and Matisse's emotional color. For Higgins, a significant meeting in Paris was with the American artist Walter Ufer, a rough, blunt man who also had lived in Chicago. Higgins was a shy, retiring person and Ufer was an aggressive extrovert, but they got along well, attracted perhaps by their different natures. They shared a mutual antagonism for academic subject matter. Though they had sought academic instruction, they regretted the lack of international recognition for American art and agreed that their country needed an identifiable art of its own.

In 1914, when he returned to Chicago, Higgins was offered a commission to do a landscape of Taos by Carter H. Harrison Jr., a wealthy buyer of his work who had been a long-time mayor of the city. Carter paid Higgins' way to Taos for the painting trip and underwrote his expenses. He did the same for Walter Ufer.

The reputation of the original six Taos artists was well known in Chicago, where their work was frequently on exhibit, and Higgins was anxious to see the village for himself. By the time he arrived, 16 years after Phillips and Blumenschein, Taos had become a recognized, if distant, art center.

Ernest Blumenschein, remembering his first meeting with Higgins, described him to Bickerstaff: "I gathered from his good breeding, soft-spoken voice, and gentle manner that his boyhood was uneventful. He was not a strong, virile character like Ufer, but one of hesitating, sensitive nature." Blumenschein also saw Higgins as a dreamer rather than a realist: "Higgins felt out his compositions with a broad, sweeping style and masses of color *en rapport.* He had a painter's style."

First Higgins went to Santa Fe where he met Sheldon Parsons, unofficial greeter of visiting artists to New Mexico. There he stayed a brief time and was entertained by the widower Parsons and his young teenage daughter Sara, who was his hostess. Shortly afterward, Higgins continued his trip to Taos. In 1915 he was invited to join the Taos Society of Artists.

Taos Landscape. *Oil, 24 x 27" (61 x 69 cm). Collection Mrs. J.R. Modrall.*

Photo Jonathan A. Meyers

Victor Higgins at work with the Rio Grande Gorge in the far distance.

IN 1916, TWO YEARS after Higgins had moved to Taos, the clouds of war drove Mabel Dodge from her salon in Paris back to America. Mabel Dodge Luhan was a stimulator of events and a generous sponsor who aided others. She and her husband Maurice Sterne had traveled to Taos in search of a remote romantic environment. (Though Maurice Sterne stayed only two years, it was he who invited Andrew Dasburg—and Cubism—to Taos.) After Mabel Dodge divorced Sterne, she married Taos Indian Tony Luhan and remained in Taos, a magnet to the talented.

The original six artists who lived in Taos were less affected by this dramatic woman than was Victor Higgins. He became a part of her circle and she also provided a house for him to live in. Higgins' association with the 'salon group' is evidence of a turn of mind that took pleasure in a more contemporary exploration of aesthetics than appealed to the other artists.

At first his paintings continued to be set pieces. Elegant and increasingly spare, they featured Indian figures in repose. But he made an effort to vary the focus of his paintings. Two of his best-known early Taos periods oils, *Fiesta Day* and *Indian Girl With Parrot*, are closeups of the major figures with an interesting background visible. Although painted in a classic manner, the color in these paintings is slightly brighter than his dun-colored academic palette. It is noteworthy that Higgins was never an illustrator. Always an "easel painter," he dispensed with the detail that is characteristic of illustration and concentrated on composition.

Taos, with its fresh pictorial possibilities, deeply satisfied him. He described his reaction to the West in a statement for the Babcock Galleries in 1920, in which he revealed the cosmopolitan references in his mind and the rather flamboyant quality of his vocabulary:

"The West is composite and it fascinates me. In the West are forests as luxurious as the forests of Fontainebleau or Lebanon: desert lands as alluring as The Sahara; and mountains most mysterious. Cañons and mesa that reveal the construction of the earth, with walls as fantastic as façades of Dravidian Temples. An architecture, also fast disappear-

ing, as homogenous as the structures of Palestine and the northern coast of Africa; and people as old as the peoples of history; with customs and costumes as ancient as their traditions. And all this is not the shifting of playhouse scenes but the erosion and growth of thousands of years, furrowed for centuries by Western rains, dried by Western winds and baked by Western suns. Nearly all that the world has, the West has in nature, fused with its own eternal self."

In 1919 Victor Higgins married Sara Parsons. He was 35, and she was 18. Their first home was one provided by Mabel Dodge Luhan. Later they rented a house on Ledoux Street, right across from the Blumenschein house, a long series of rooms attached together in the adobe style.

Primitive facilities were the custom in Taos, but other aspects of life, particularly conversation, were of a high order. As a member of the Taos Society of Artists and as a friend of Mabel Dodge Luhan's circle, Victor Higgins was a favored raconteur with an Irish gift for storytelling. His young wife Sara found the social side of her shared life enjoyable and was especially fond of Mabel Dodge Luhan, who was her good friend. Sara recalled Higgins as a "fabulous public speaker in demand in the East for his lectures on art." But face to face, she said, he became "mumbly-bumbly," not much given to small talk.

Higgins suffered, even in his 30s, from an ulcer. He drove himself and was a preoccupied artist. He also had strong opinions about the role of woman as helpmate to the husband. The marriage was one of incompatibles, for Sara Parsons Higgins was a spirited, talented, athletic girl who required outlets for her prodigious abilities and had always enjoyed an adult, stimulating life with her father. The marriage ended in 1924, much to Higgins' sorrow. He loved his beautiful, red-haired wife and cherished their daughter Joan, born in 1922. Their relationship became that of dear friends, without rancor, and extended to include Sara's second husband of over 40 years, Robert Mack. The influence of Sara's powerfully discerning eye during their brief marriage was important in the career of Victor Higgins, for she steered him toward a more stark style, away from a tendency to theatrics and decoration.

HIGGINS WAS a handsome gray-eyed, brown-haired man of medium build. His mustache was always trim and his head neatly barbered. In his studio or on location he always painted while dressed formally in a white shirt and tie. As a matter of fact, his so-called "Little Gems," which were painted outdoors in all kinds of weather, were sometimes painted by Higgins in hat, suit, and coat. Laura Gilpin once photographed him on a painting trip in this city costume sitting under the trunk lid of his car. Higgins apparently saw no incongruity between his professionally formal attire and the usual messiness of a painters gear because he himself was so fastidious in his handling of paint.

An abortive marriage in 1928 to a Texas heiress was his only other foray into matrimony. However, for many years he enjoyed the tender, dignified, friendship of Eleanor Kissel, a well-to-do, talented artist who lived in Taos. Though Higgins lived as a bachelor most of his life, he was not a recluse. As a teacher, he gave concise, useful critiques, and he helped many young artists.

Dean Porter, his biographer, traces a second Taos period in Higgins' work that began around 1920. He selects the only abstract oil Higgins ever painted, *Circumferences* (page 88) as a breakthrough, revealing the mystic nature of the artist. In this painting, arcs and pastel colorations appear to demark the path of bombs and trajectories of bullets over an anguished war-torn edge of earth under a distant moon. The painting, owned by the University of Notre Dame, was Higgins' reaction to World War I, or perhaps his fear of World War II. It could not have been painted by any of the other artists in the Taos Society of Artists and it is atypical of Higgins, too, but it does show his capacity to remove himself from subject matter as such and become more purely a creator of a painting. However it is analyzed, after 1920 there is a change in brushwork, color, and subject matter that enlivens Higgins' work, separating it still further from that of other TSA artists.

Brushwork in his earlier work was free and juicy, but in later works it takes on a more graphic quality. Higgins often made patterns of adjacent bold strokes in a manner that seems to relate to Cézanne. He searched for the basic form of the nearby mountain and rendered it as a series of diagonal slabs. These he painted in dynamically angled strokes charged with energy. Clouds became flat strata of varying lengths receding in space. The valley became a series of stripes or a rickrack of color. The essentials of form gradually took precedence over accidents of appearance.

It is hard to judge how much he was affected by Andrew Dasburg, who came to Taos in 1917. But Dasburg shared the Cubist approach with those who were interested, and Higgins was among them.

Meeting John Marin in 1929 and painting with him on fishing trips came at a perfectly timed moment in Higgins' life. He had been moving toward simplification in his work, and he enjoyed watercolor, Marin's favored medium, as much as oil. There is a pronounced kinship between Higgins' watercolors and those Marin did in New Mexico in their reduction and calligraphic symbolism. It is difficult, however, to determine whose influence was more powerful, for Higgins was in his own habitat and had a staccato style before he met Marin.

Gateway. *Oil, 30 x 30′ (76 x 76 cm). McAdoo Galleries, Inc., Woodrow Wilson Fine Arts, Santa Fe.*

Taos Pueblo. Oil, 30 x 30" (76 x 75 cm). Collection Mr. and Mrs. Gerald P. Peters.

O F THE EARLY TAOS ARTISTS, Higgins alone excelled in watercolor. Among his many varied substantial contributions to American art, his watercolors add greatly to the development of the medium, though they have still received less than their rightful recognition.

The older he grew, the more Higgins was able to do with the least means. He developed private schema for pine trees, clouds, earth, and adobes that rank him with Charles Burchfield in creative expression in watercolor. On dry, rough paper he dragged his brush to allow the greatest amount of sparkle in a series of paintings done during the '30s when he blossomed as a watercolorist.

One of the most widely reproduced of Higgins' oils is *Winter Funeral* (page 88). Painted in 1931 and owned by the Harwood Foundation in Taos, it was described by Mabel Dodge Luhan as "a painting that many have seen and never forgotten." In this oil, Higgins viewed the snow-covered Taos Valley from a vantage point with the baseline of the mountain, which divides *Winter Funeral* in half horizontally. Above, the greenish-gray multitriangular mountains brood under heavy snow-laden clouds; below, the snow is blemished by dark, flat shapes of funeral wagons, coffins, and cars. In the immediate foreground is the edge of a frozen stream and a few trees. Higgins has devised a framework for the scene that cuts each corner and forms a diamond superimposed on the rectangular canvas. The effect is to squeeze the picture back into deeper space, accordion fashion, and further isolate it. The funeral is made pathetically unimportant and small when compared to the large scale of the setting.

Higgins relieved his cool, limited palette with just a few touches of warm reds and ochres on the mountain, in the sky, and on the trees. It is a lonely, harsh, and haunting scene, a complete statement that stands as one of the finest paintings in the history of American landscape. It also marks, for Higgins, an end to the figure in landscape and the beginning of landscape for its own sake, a subject that the other artists in Taos did not paint with the same concentration.

In addition to his landscapes, Higgins shared two other interests in common with Cézanne. One was in still lifes, especially of flowers, on slightly tilted tabletops, and the other was in figure studies done in the studio, whose power rests on design and abstraction.

Victor Higgins had a distinguished career. In 1921, after winning many major prizes in Chicago and New York, he was elected an Associate of the National Academy of Design. He was also one of the Taos artists asked to paint murals for the state capitol of Missouri in Jefferson City. In 1935 he was elected to full membership in the National Academy. Though his painting sales were not as steady as some of the other artists' in Taos, he aligned himself with a shrewd Chicago dealer who once had his work placed in some new homes, a move that netted Higgins a check for over $10,000. In his later years, he participated in fewer exhibitions. Though he did not achieve the popular success accorded to Couse, Sharp, Blumenschein, and Ufer, he did enjoy esteem and recognition from the art community.

I N THE LAST FIVE YEARS of his life, from the mid- to the late '40s, he did a series of fresh, small landscapes, his "Little Gems," that synthesized his proficiency with the brush and his intensified vision. Ernest Blumenschein recalls them in Bickerstaff's *Pioneer Artists of Taos:*

"His last group of pictures I shall never forget. They were done on sketching trips around Taos Valley and in the Rio Grande Canon. In them was the best Higgins quality, a lyrical charm added to his lovely color. His art had developed in [an] intellectual side through his adventure with Dynamic Symmetry and other abstract angles. Not that he used mechanical formulas. He always had, as do most good artists, an instinct that guided his form structure. . . . And he put all he had into this dozen of small canvases. They must have been about eighteen [inches] wide by ten inches high. All works of love: love of his simple subjects and of his craftsmanship. These pictures had the 'extra something' that the right artist can put into his work when he is 'on his toes.' "

These "Little Gems" have become the most sought after of Higgins' work. Not just once, but time after time, he created paintings with economy and power about which a viewer could truthfully say there is not a stroke out of place nor unnecessary to the whole.

While dining with his friends, the Thomas Benrimos,

Higgins was stricken with a heart attack and died in Taos on August 23, 1949.

Victor Higgins was articulate about art. In an interview with Ina Sizer Cassidy in 1932 he clarified his ideas and career: "The trouble with most people is that they see too much with the eye only and not enough with the inner eye, the emotions. . . . And they take art on, especially in the women's clubs and art societies, too much as entertainment, not enough as serious scientific study. A painter paints a canvas not because he wants to make a 'picture' as that he wants to solve a problem. A problem in form, in construction, design, if you prefer that term, in color harmonies.

"The term *reality* is greatly misunderstood. It does not mean the ability to copy nature, as most people seem to think, it means more than that, the *reality* of being. The difference between the modernistic and the romantic form of art, as I see it, is the architectural basis. The modern painter . . . *builds* his picture, he does not merely paint it. He has his superstructure, his foundation, just as an architect has for his buildings."

When he was asked why he liked to paint in Taos, he spoke of its color and added, "And besides this, there is a constant call here to create something."

Pablita Passes. Oil, 40 x 43" (102 x 109 cm). Collection Museum of Fine Arts, Museum of New Mexico, Santa Fe. On permanent loan from Robert L. Tobin.

WALTER UFER
Diamond in the Rough

ALTER UFER WAS BORN in Louisville, Kentucky, in 1876. His family was German and there was an atmosphere of liberalism which Ufer described to Ina Sizer Cassidy as one "almost of radicalism" in the home (*New Mexico Magazine*, 1933). This radicalism clung to him as a characteristic that distinguishes Ufer from the other artists in Taos.

Mayrion Bisttram, widow of Taos artist Emil Bisttram, said of him, "Ufer was a gnome. His legs had not grown normally but his chest was very broad and solid, and he walked with a bit of a stoop." Victor White referred to "his fierce lantern jaw, his detective-sergeant eyes behind the steel-rimmed glasses, and a voice that could swoop from pianissimo to the thunder of Jove" (*The Taos News*, 1968).

Ufer's antic appearance was exaggerated by his clothes. He had a fondness for pieces of military uniform bought for low prices at the surplus store. He wore a uniform jacket, breeches, hat, and puttees. A chain-smoker of cigarettes, Ufer had the usually raspy voice that goes with the habit. He also was a heavy drinker for many years.

He was a brilliant and tormented man with a paradoxical nature. On the one hand, he was a gruff person who liked to shock the shockable with foul language; on the other, he was a gentle man who loved children. One of his kindnesses was to buy all the chances on a punchboard at the drugstore, which insured that he would win the prize box of candy, and to distribute his "winnings" among the children on the plaza in Taos.

On his studio door, across the road from his house, he had painted a sign in big letters "KEEP OUT. T.N.T., EXPLOSIVE" and so effectively kept visitors away at a time when there were no commercial galleries in Taos and patrons had to visit the artists' studios to buy from them directly. Yet, if the children could stay quiet, he would sometimes let them come in to watch him paint. Ufer had no children of his own.

Some of his abundant emotion he showered on the Taos Indians, and they remembered him as a hero. During the dreadful flu epidemic of 1918-1919, Ufer worked night and day alongside the only doctor, administering to the victims who were being treated in the schoolhouse.

Ufer was an ardent and active socialist, not from a political stance, but from his belief in the cause of laborers. When coal miners went out on strike in Madrid, New Mexico, Ufer canvassed the town to collect money for them. Some of those who found his language offensive were also turned off by his liberalism.

There is a legend, probably true, that a political confrere of Ufer's smuggled Leon Trotsky north from his exile in Mexico and brought him to visit Ufer in the dark of night. Another visitor who came to see him was Emile Gauguin,

son of Paul Gauguin, whose Danish mother was a friend of Mrs. Ufer's family in Denmark.

The writer Victor White, who met Ufer several years before the artist's death, was himself a guest at a memorable dinner. He described it wittily. Ufer had said to him: " 'You like rabbit stew made with white wine, the way the French cook it? My wife knows how to do it. I've got some interesting people coming. If you want to come, come over around six'—but it sounded forbidding.

"The rabbit stew was memorable, but the rest of the evening more so. The 'interesting people' turned out to be the Communist candidate for governor of the State, fresh out of jail over in Las Vegas, and the elegant young Schilling spice fortune heiress. No less improbable combination would have satisfied Walter's sense of drama."

Wherever there was interest and excitement, Ufer was sure to be found. In the last year of his life, Ufer was fighting against legalized gambling in New Mexico.

Movies were one of the few entertainments in Taos. Ufer, Blumenschein, and Couse were regulars at the little theater near the corner of the plaza. When a pretty girl flicked on the screen in the drafty hall, Ufer usually made an audible and ribald comment to Blumy, seated somewhere down in front. Their banter is among the lighter memories people still recall of that period.

For all of his colorful personal characteristics, the most marked attribute of the man was his professionalism as an artist. Ufer began his extensive education in boyhood when his father, an engraver of gunstocks, apprenticed him to a commercial lithographer. After a time, the lithographer decided to return home to Hamburg, Germany. The 17-year-old Ufer had no funds, but he followed his master by stowing away on a ship. After being discovered, he was put to work peeling potatoes in the galley.

It was the custom for an apprentice who had completed his studies to become a journeyman. That meant he would travel about from place to place offering his skill in various towns until it was perfected. In another year or so he would be a recognized master. Ufer was on his journey working as a printer and engraver when he arrived in Dresden. There he felt such a lure of the fine arts that he enrolled at the Dresden Royal Academy and the Royal Applied Art School. On his return to the States he supported himself as a commercial engraver and lithographer, first in Louisville where he was head of the art department for the *Louisville Courier-Journal*, and then in Chicago where he worked for Armour and Company. Ufer's exposure to European academies had fed his desire to paint for exhibitions, which he entered in Chicago, where he was given attention for his portraits.

Water Carriers (Isleta, N.M.). Oil, 30 x 30″ (76 x 76 cm). Carter Harrison Collection. Fred A. Rosenstock, Denver.

IN NEW YORK, Ufer met Mary Monrad Fredericksen, an accomplished and well-bred artist-musician of Danish extraction whose grandfather had been Prime Minister of Denmark. She became his wife and the couple went off to Europe and studied together at the Royal Academy in Munich. Here Ufer's path crossed those of Victor Higgins and E. Martin Hennings. Like the other two men, one of his teachers was Walter Thor.

The Ufers traveled and painted in Paris, Rome, and North Africa before they returned to Chicago. Both in Europe and in Chicago, Ufer's draftsmanship became known and was highly praised, and Carter H. Harrison Jr. soon approached Ufer with an offer to underwrite a painting trip to Taos. Ufer later recalled Harrison's contribution to art: "Carter Harrison has done more for American art, for Taos art, New Mexican art, than any other man I know. He has always been a 'booster' and a buyer, which is the best kind of 'booster,' and has made it possible for a number of outstanding American artists to succeed."

Ufer accepted Harrison's offer and traveled to Taos in 1914. When he arrived he exclaimed: "God's country! I expect to live and die here." He was 38 years old, and a seasoned artist with a strong, academic style.

The landscape, the Indians, and the ambience of Taos captured Ufer as it had other members of the Taos Society of Artists. He joined the society in 1915, its seventh member. At first Ufer painted in Taos only during the summer and lived in New York in the winter, but he later moved permanently to Taos.

Taos vitally affected Ufer's academic approach to painting. He lightened his palette in response to the brilliance of Taos skies, and he moved out into the landscape with his easel. Ufer traveled around Taos in his car as he searched for his compositions in nature itself. He was a disciple of Dynamic Symmetry, a compositional theory popular at the time, but he did not impose its principles on his subjects. Instead, he found his own dynamic compositional structure. Often he chose circular directional lines within a scene and then painted the scene as he saw it.

Many of Ufer's Indian pictures are of figures in landscape. He once wrote a catalog entry for Babcock Galleries about his work, saying: "I choose my motifs and take my models to my motifs. I design the painting there. I do not make small sketches of my models first but put my full vitality and enthusiasm into the one and original painting. Studio work dulls the mind and the artist's palette. I do not use the camera, in fact I know nothing of photography.

"A large painting must have the same strength and freshness that a small sketch has, and to make a large painting you must go at it just the same way as if you were making a small one. . . . I paint one motif only once and drop it seeking another."

Ufer also wrote: "This country will never be painted out for it has an infinite variety of moods and types" (*El Palacio*, August 1916).

Cowboys and Adobe. *Oil on canvas, 25 x 30" (64 x 76 cm) Carter Harrison Collection. Fred A. Rosenstock, Denver.*

Ufer's Jim: Jim Mirabal shortly before his death at 92(?).

UFER STUDIED the Indian way of life with intense curiosity and developed lasting friendships with his Indian neighbors. One of Ufer's favorite models was Jim Mirabal, a Taos Indian who was also known as "Ufer's Jim." Whether or not he had money at the time, Ufer managed to look after Mirabal and his family. If necessary, he borrowed the money to give to him and later paid it back when he made a sale. It was Ufer who paid for the first room in the Mirabal adobe home at the pueblo. Mirabal lived into his nineties and always remembered his patron. "We were like brothers," he said not long before he died in 1976.

Ufer's paintings of Mirabal and other models in the sunny landscape of Taos Valley brought him many successes. He was the first New Mexican painter to win a prize in the Carnegie International. The major awards in that exhibition were usually given to European artists. When Ufer won a third prize, all the artists in Taos shared in the pride of his selection.

He also won the Chicago Art Institute's First Logan Prize in 1917; and the Martin C. Cahn Prize two times, in 1916 and 1922. He won the William M. R. French Gold Medal in 1922. In the same year he was named juror of the Pennsylvania Academy of the Fine Arts. In 1923 he won that school's Temple Gold Medal. He won the National Academy of Design First Altman Prize in 1917 and again in 1921; and he was awarded the Second Altman Prize, the Isidor Gold Medal, and he was elected to membership in the academy, all in 1926. He was also a member of the Chicago Society of Artists, the Salmagundi Club, and a Fellow of the Royal Society of Artists.

Ufer became famous and his shows were reviewed with serious attention. In a special issue of *El Palacio* on "The Santa Fe-Taos Art Colony: Walter Ufer" (August 1916, pp. 75-81), one writer observed with prescience, "In all of Mr. Ufer's work we are aware of an abundant and forceful energy. Whether it be thoughtfully or temperamentally directed." In that same issue another reviewer said, "Ufer . . . has thrown a new glamour about scenes that are familiar. He has done it with the sure stroke of a master. . . ."

Ufer's oils brought the West to life for many fans who cherished their American flavor. "He conveys to us an enjoyment of the sunlight and the air and the freedom of the desert and the mountains such as the Indians themselves must feel," the *El Palacio* article reported.

He was included in the Venice Biennial in 1924 and in the U.S. Exhibition in Paris in 1919, one of seven New Mexico painters in that important show. He was represented in New York and enjoyed many sales.

When the sales abruptly stopped, due to a general economic downturn and to his drinking problem, he sent his gold medals to the mint in Denver to be melted down into currency and was outraged to learn they were only gold-plated. He had to sell paintings for a few hundred dollars that had been selling for thousands in his hey-day.

Ufer's painting method is better known than that of the other Taos founders. Perhaps that is because it has more of the uniquely personal about it, or because Ufer's former pupil, Regina Tatum Cooke, has documented it. At any rate, this is how he worked:

Once he had chosen a subject and posed his model, Ufer secured his easel with cord to a handy nearby rock and covered the back of his stretcher bars with black cloth so the sun would not shine through the canvas. Then he began to draw with a 4B hard drawing pencil, always keeping the dynamics of his composition clearly in mind.

His next step was to go over all the drawing lines with a smooth mixture of permanent blue and turpentine. He used this mix to lay in the shadows, too. After it dried he erased the pencil lines to make a "cleaner canvas."

Ufer painted from the top of the canvas straight down to the bottom and rarely needed to retouch any of it to bring it into harmony. "Treat things as a whole," he often said. Figure or ground, they had to be treated as one. "The horse becomes a part of the mesa and takes on the colors of the mesa," he would explain.

Though his draftsmanship is frequently praised, his color is also notable. There is a greenish cast to his light and a sparkle to his shadows that are strictly Ufer's own and that give a freshness to his paintings.

UFER WAS SPARING in his use of details, usually reserving them for the immediate foreground. However, he painted true portraits of his models within the landscape motif, carrying on the skill he had become known for in his Chicago days. Such accuracy in the models' faces gives the impression of detail, but actually comes from his precise, accurate drawing with the brush, despite the overall broadness of his style. He was a deft, sure painter.

Ufer's palette of Weimar paints from Germany consisted of: verte emeraude, permanent green light, cerulean blue, cobalt blue, permanent blue, alizarin crimson, vermilion, yellow ochre, cadmium yellows, burnt sienna, and white. He did not use black, but simulated it with a mixture of permanent blue and burnt sienna.

Regina Tatum Cooke remembers that he was persnickety about his brushes. He washed them every day with Ivory soap and warm water. When she studied with him between 1934 and 1936, she worked on two paintings a day, one in the morning and another in the afternoon—Ufer's own custom. Before lunch and again in the afternoon at the end of the painting day, she washed her brushes with Ivory soap, just as he did.

Ufer took very few pupils. Cooke recalls his generosity. He charged her only $36 a month and critiqued her work every day. She says simply, "He was a wonderful teacher."

In the early years, Mary Ufer was content to stay in Taos each summer and leave the rest of the year for the sophistication of New York; but after the Ufers settled permanently in Taos, its confinement began to chafe her. She gave up her own painting, but she put together some slide talk shows about the Taos artists and took them on promotional tours to clubs and gatherings around the country.

No doubt Ufer's drinking also became a burden to her. In later years they were separated for longer periods while Mary was in the East, and Ufer was a resident bachelor. Mary had taught a young Taos girl to cook, and she remained loyal to Ufer. Although a happily married woman without need of work, she continued to cook for him—if he had any food. There were times when he lived on bread,

cheese, and coffee, and would share even that little if someone poorer than he came to his table.

When things were at their worst, Ufer borrowed money. William Klauer, owner of a rotary snowplow factory in Dubuque, Iowa, was a devoted collector of Ufer's work. Whenever he bought a painting, Ufer would go around and pay off his debts.

The largest collection of Ufer's work belongs to Lewis Ruskin of Phoenix, Arizona, who has donated or loaned the paintings to the Phoenix Art Museum and to the Arizona State University Museum. Other paintings are in numerous public collections throughout the country, including the Anschutz Collection, Denver; the Stark Museum of Orange, Texas; and the Gilcrease Institute of Tulsa, Oklahoma.

Ufer's life was marked by more sharp contrasts of good and bad fortune than was that of the other Taos pioneers. There was a year when he earned over $50,000 from his work. For several years running, in the '20s, he had a large income. He spent it lavishly and enjoyed such extravagances as a private railroad car on a trip to Chicago. He seemed to live life to the hilt and then to suffer the inevitable depressions that followed. Despite his intemperate life, both his friends and his wife remained faithful to him. They convinced him to enter a sanitarium in Colorado and take the cure. Afterward he never drank again.

In August, 1936, Ufer suffered an attack of appendicitis. Friends made a pallet for him in the back of E. Martin Hennings' Ford and they drove him as rapidly as possible to St. Vincent's Hospital in Santa Fe. It is thought that Ufer's appendix burst on the way to the hospital. This was before the days of wonder drugs, and the doctors were unable to save him. Ufer died three days later.

After his death, his wife Mary returned for a memorial service held in his studio. Around a table with a bouquet of white roses on it, one by one, the artists spoke of Ufer. Kenneth Adams made one of the speeches in praise of his first friend in Taos. At Ufer's request, he was cremated and his ashes scattered in an arroyo near Mabel Dodge Luhan's house, where he had loved to paint.

Walter Ufer in surplus Army puttees and pants at work in Taos. The Lucinda Martin Iliff Collection, Kit Carson Memorial Foundation, Taos.

in the Foothills. *Oil, 20 x 16" (51 x 41 cm). The Santa Fe Collection of Southwestern Art.*

William Herbert Dunton

My Children. *Oil, 50 x 60" (127 x 152 cm). Collection Museum of Fine Arts, Museum of New Mexico, Santa Fe.*

Timberline. *Oil, 30 x 30" (76 x 76 cm). Collection Ivan H. Dunton.*

Vivian on Horse with Cowboy. *Oil, 30 x 24" (76 x 61 cm). Private collection.*

orse Wrangler. Oil, 25 x 20¼'' (64 x 51 cm). The San Antonio Art League.

Elk in the Aspens. *Oil, 13¾ x 13¾" (35 x 35 cm). Collection Harrison Eiteljorg.*

June on Taos Creek. *Oil, 13¾ x 13¾" (35 x 35 cm). Collection Harrison Eiteljorg.*

Old Texas. *Oil, 28 x 39" (71 x 99 cm). The San Antonio Art League.*

Indian Composition. *Oil, 38 x 32" (97 x 81 cm). Eugene B. Adkins Collection.*

The Sentinel. *Oil, 18 x 20″ (46 x 51 cm). Fenn Galleries, Ltd., Santa Fe.*

Ledoux Street, Taos. *Oil, 13 x 18″ (33 x 76 cm). Eugene B. Adkins Collection.*

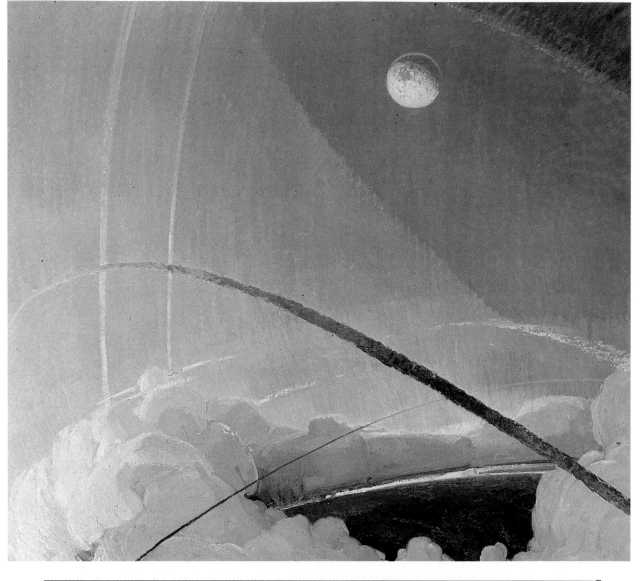

Winter Funeral. *Oil, 47 x 60″ (119 x 152 cm). Collection the Harwood Foundation, University of New Mexico, Taos.*

Mountains and Valleys. *Oil, 40 x 40" (102 x 102 cm). Collection Harrison Eiteljorg.*

orm Approaching Adobe.
atercolor, 19 x 24" (48 x 61 cm).
urtesy Gerald P. Peters,
nta Fe, New Mexico.

Sundown, *1916. Oil, 30 x 25" (76 x 51 cm). Carter Harrison Collection. Courtesy Fred A. Rosenstock, Denver.*

Desert Trail. *Oil, 25 x 25″ (64 x 64 cm). The Santa Fe Collection of Southwestern Art.*

Chance Encounter. *Oil, 20 x 25″ (51 x 64 cm). Collection Museum of Fine Arts, Museum of New Mexico, Santa Fe.*

Jim and His Daughter. *Oil, 40 x 50¼" (102 x 128 cm). Fenn Galleries, Ltd., Santa Fe.*

Desert Trail Near Taos, *1917. Oil, 30 x 30″ (76 x 76 cm).*
The Anschutz Collection.

Daughter of San Juan Pueblo. *Oil, 30″ x 25″ (76 x 51 cm). Exhibited Panama Pacific*
Exposition. Carter Harrison Collection. Courtesy Fred A. Rosenstock, Denver.

Taos Girls. *Oil, 30 x 30″ (76 x 76 cm). The Santa Fe Collection of Southwestern Art.*

Taos Autumn. *Oil, 30 x 24″ (76 x 61 cm). Brandywine Galleries Ltd., Albuquerq*

Going to the Waterhole, Santa Clara. *Oil, 25 x 30' (64 x 76 cm). Collection Harrison Eiteljorg.*

CATHERINE CARTER CRITCHER
Honored Visitor

Nova Scotia Fisherman. *Oil, 26½ x 26½'' (67 x 67 cm). Collection Mr. and Mrs. Toy Dixon Savage, Jr.*

IN THE SUMMER OF 1922 the Washington, D.C. artist Catherine Carter Critcher arrived in Taos for her first visit. Her friend and colleague C. Powell Minnegrade, Director of the Corcoran Gallery, had supplied her with two letters of introduction, one to Victor Higgins and the other to Walter Ufer. She wrote a chatty account to Minnegrade on August 30th:

"Your letters have worked like magic. We, Mrs. Chase and I, first called upon Mr. Higgins & his very attractive wife. They are both charming. Soon we were asked to come in the evening & have coffee with them & we had a great Art talk. Next we were asked to his studio to see his pictures. They were of unusual interest & beauty.

"We were told by several here that Ufer was very unapproachable & one never knew just what sort of treatment they would receive from him. So we trembled at the thought of calling, finally went, he fairly fell all over himself with what seemed genuine pleasure. He took your letter & said 'Now it surely was nice of Minnigerode [Critcher's joking spelling of the name as Ufer had pronounced it] to do this' & again 'how nice of him.' They were at supper & would not accept our refusal to have dessert & tea with them, so we accepted. Then came a deluge of pictures & we feasted. Soon he called & then asked us to come & see his pictures by daylight. . . .

"Taos is unlike any place God ever made I believe & therein is charm & no place could be more conducive to work. There are models galore & no phones. The artists all live in these attractive funny little adobe houses away from the world, food, foes & friends. So the combination is unique. Am working full steam . . ." (Catherine Carter Critcher Correspondence File, Corcoran Gallery of Art, Washington, D.C.).

Critcher so enjoyed Taos that she continued to make summer visits and to write the news to Minnegrade. The mail zipped back and forth at a rapid clip between Taos and Washington—hers to Dear Powell and his to Dear Miss Kate. A letter Critcher wrote on July 10 was received by Minnegrade on July 14 and his response was dated July 15. It is doubtful that such speedy deliveries could be matched today, and it sheds a light on how well the Taos artists were able to keep up their careers via the U.S. Post Office.

In 1924 Minnegrade interceded for Critcher with the Director of the Maryland Institute in Baltimore, a Mr. Bement, to hire Critcher for their faculty at approximately $2000 per year. The advantages of the job impressed Critcher and in her response, dated July 19, she wrote: "The position appeals to me quite strongly, in case of accepting it think I shall give up my private classes in Wash[ington]. While these classes are large & profitable the business end requires much time & thought which I should be able to eliminate by taking the Maryland Inst. position & not have to teach such a variety of subjects."

In the same letter, Critcher also shared her pleasure at some good news: "You will be pleased, I know, to hear that a letter just rec'd from Mr. Couse informs me that I have been unanimously elected to active membership in the Taos Society of Artists. It's nice to be the first & only woman in it. I am feeling very good about it."

She also confided some gossip she thought Minnegrade would be interested in and that had rocked Taos: "You may have heard that Mrs. Victor Higgins has left Mr. Higgins. She has taken a home in Santa Fe and started legal proceedings for a divorce. Everyone here says that he has been kindness & generosity itself to her."

Critcher was a genteel woman of 56 at the time, steeped in the code of her class on the Eastern seaboard. She did not become so fully a part of Taos that she could share the understanding for the spirited, beautiful, red-haired, Sara Parsons Higgins that Mabel Dodge Luhan felt for her young friend. But Critcher prized her membership in the Taos Society of Artists throughout her long career.

Oscar E. Berninghaus. *Oil, 30 x 25" (76 x 64 cm). The National Academy of Design.*

CRITCHER WAS BORN just a few years after the Civil War ended, on September 13, 1868. She lived 96 years until June 11, 1964. Her parents were Judge John and Elizabeth Whiting Critcher of Westmoreland County, Virginia. The Critchers were among the First Families of Virginia, dating back to colonial times. After a gracious upbringing, Catherine devoted her life to art. She never married, but is remembered as petite and personable. Her conversation was lively and she had a ready smile. It has been said that she was the darling of the Taos Society.

At the turn of the century, Critcher was a student, albeit a mature one, at the Corcoran School of Art in Washington, D.C. She went to Paris for further study with Richard Miller and Charles Hoffbauer at the Académie Julien. Critcher lived well, but always worked hard to provide for herself. In Paris she was able to establish Cour Critcher, an atelier in which Richard Miller was the instructor and a partner. The studio and its classes were open to American artists who could work there at modest cost without a language barrier. She maintained the studio from 1905 until her return to Washington in 1909.

The Corcoran School appointed her Instructor in Antique Art that year for an annual salary of $450, raised eventually to $500. When she resigned on June 1, 1919, she opened her own school at 3 St. Matthew's Alley, a short street behind St. Matthew's Catholic Church where artists such as sculptor George Julian Zolnay and Viktor Flambeau (pseudonym for Gertrude Richardson Brigham, art historian, world traveler, and art critic for the *Washington Post*) had their studios in reconditioned stables and garages. Critcher and Clara Hill, a sculptor friend she knew in Paris, continued to operate the Critcher-Hill School of Art at various addresses on Connecticut Avenue. Catherine's older sister, Lula Critcher, was manager of the successful school, later called the Critcher School of Painting and Applied Art.

During the Depression she also ran a summer school in the rugged Virginia mountains. Tuition for the four-week course was only $25; room and board were $15.

Critcher was a founding member of the Society of Washington Artists and won a bronze and a silver medal in their shows. She was a regular contributor to the Corcoran juried exhibitions until late in her life. One of the paintings she exhibited was awarded the purchase prize of $500. In 1960 the Corcoran sold the painting *Light Lightning* for a reported $28,700.

During the '20s and '30s Critcher's portraits brought her fame. Her portrait of Woodrow Wilson is owned by Princeton University where he was once president. The National Academy of Design owns her portrait of Oscar E. Berninghaus. The San Antonio Art League also owns her work. She painted portraits of 20 generals, including George Marshall and Mark Clark. Her *War Chief* is owned by the Philadelphia Museum of Art.

Every summer for a number of years, Critcher lived in an art colony. She belonged to the Provincetown, Massachusetts Art Association and exhibited with them until 1926. Among her paintings shown were florals, landscapes, and portraits. In Taos she was excited by the variety of people, and her paintings of Indians and Spanish-Americans were popular.

She was a superior designer. Kenneth Adams, after looking a long while at her *Taos Hoop Dancer*, called it a "painter's painting." It is an intricately planned composition on a bold scale. Each area of the pattern fits into a relationship with the circular hoop and the square format. Outlines are important and they function as a lyrical tracery in the work. Color is controlled and somewhat arbitrary. There is a modern 20th-century look to her paintings, although they are obviously the work of an academically trained artist.

Viktor Flambeau wrote of her neighbor, "Miss Critcher is always painting. Her work is dominant and positive, with nothing negative or sentimental, though she herself is very feminine."

After her five visits to Taos, Critcher spent the summer of 1926 in Taxco, Mexico. In later years her summers were spent in New Orleans, the Gaspé Peninsula, and Gloucester, Massachusetts.

For all her success, Critcher has received little attention as a member of the Taos Society of Artists. Possibly this is because her residence in the village was so limited. Taos provided her with a wealth of subject matter and friendships, but she did not feel the same desire to base her career in the outpost as did the other members of the group for whom Taos was home.

Washington, D.C. was Critcher's point of reference and it was there that she had entrée into society, which insured the success of her portrait career. Nonetheless, Taos gave her a signal honor. Many artists made their homes in Taos during the '20s, but only 11 of them were ever asked to join the Taos Society of Artists—and one of these was Catherine Carter Critcher.

E. MARTIN HENNINGS
A Love Story

Courtesy Mrs. E.M. Hennings.

E. MARTIN HENNINGS, the second youngest member of the Taos Society of Artists, was born February 5, 1886, in Penns Grove, New Jersey, and grew up in Chicago. His father, of German descent, was a skilled craftsman.

Helen Hennings Winton, writing about her father for *The Taos News* in 1968, said: "I can remember from my own very early childhood hearing the story of Dad's visit to the Art Institute when he was about thirteen. So awed and impressed was he by what he saw there that he decided then that he would make art his life's work."

At 15 Hennings began Saturday classes, and in 1904 he graduated from the Institute with honors. However, he continued to study there for two more years, while working at a commercial studio painting murals for public buildings. By 1912 he had saved enough money to afford further study abroad. Franz Von Stuck, an esteemed teacher and painter in Munich, accepted Hennings as his student at the Royal Academy on the basis of his portfolio presentation. For two and a half years, Hennings studied at the Academy; his other teachers there were Walter Thor and Angelo Junk. Victor Higgins and Walter Ufer were his fellow students and friends.

Until Martin Hennings applied for his passport, he never realized that the full name on his baptismal record was Ernest Martin Hennings. Ernest was his father's name. Thereafter, he always included the initial "E" in his clearly printed signature.

When World War I started in 1914, Hennings was at risk staying in Germany, and so he returned home via Holland in 1915. At 28 he was an accomplished academic painter and a gifted draftsman with 13 years of study and professional work to his credit—yet he was not sure what he wanted to do. For a few months he painted in Gloucester, Massachusetts. Several paintings from that visit are owned by his relatives, but almost everything else from his youth was lost in a fire at the family home.

Hennings went back to painting murals at a commercial studio in Chicago. Murals are a demanding art with a long history. They give an artist scope and they provided a challenge that Hennings especially enjoyed. One of his commissions in these years was *The Ascension of Christ* for the Grace Episcopal Cathedral in Topeka, Kansas.

At the same time, Hennings maintained a studio in the Tree Studio Building, where he showed his work to interested patrons. He also entered and won prizes at the annual competitive exhibitions at the Art Institute. His work soon came to the attention of Carter H. Harrison Jr. Harrison was a prominent figure in Chicago, where he had five times been elected mayor and was a partner in an art-buying syndicate with the well-known meatpacking czar Oscar Mayer. Mayer and Harrison were sportsmen who favored Taos for their hunting trips in the mountains. Earlier they had sponsored Higgins and Ufer in their initial visits to Taos.

In 1917 Harrison approached Hennings with a similar proposal to the one he made Higgins and Ufer: If he would paint in Taos for a while, up to a year, they would guarantee the purchase of his work and support him. Harrison's offer provided Hennings with his artistic destiny. At a time of volatile stylistic changes in European art, Hennings found inspiration in a change of subject matter, while retaining his style—and a lovely, lyrical style it was.

Hennings was an outstanding draftsman and was always aware of line in his monoprints, lithographs, etchings, and drawings, as well as his paintings. The line in Hennings' compositions was often decoratively sinuous in an Art Nouveau manner. Favorite subjects were figures and trees, and he is known for his oils of Indians on horseback moving through dappled forest light. He was a sensitive painter, a classicist, with a delicate rather than a bold touch.

Indian Bake Ovens. *Lithograph, 10 x 10" (25 x 25 cm). Collection Mrs. E.M. Hennings.*

Stringing the Bow. *Etching, 8 x 10" (20 x 25 cm). Collection Robert and Judith White.*

After the Leaves Have Fallen. *Oil, 25 x 30" (64 x 76 cm). Collection Mrs. J.R. Modrall. Photo Jonathan A. Meyers.*

Hondo Canyon. *Oil, 36 x 30" (91 x 76 cm). Collection Mrs. E.M. Hennings.*

THE TAOS SCENE appealed greatly to him. He later recalled, "I constantly grew more enthusiastic over the West for I was impressed with the possibilities for landscape and figure composition. New Mexico has almost made a landscape painter out of me, although I believe my strongest work is in figures." (Reginald Fisher, "E. Martin Hennings, Artist of Taos," *El Palacio*, August 1946.)

He spent most of 1917 painting in Taos, then returned to the commercial studio in Chicago for two more years. "In 1919," he wrote, "I took stock of myself and realized my salvation was to free myself of any commercial thought and for at least three years to paint exclusively for my own development. With the idea of finding myself, I returned to Taos and worked there for five consecutive years. It was during the third year that three my paintings took prizes. Of course they brought recognition. My standpoint is that art is either good or bad and its school has not a great deal to do with it. In every picture I expect the fundamentals to be observed and these I term: draftsmanship, design, form, rhythm, color. Art must of necessity be the artist's own reaction to nature and his personal style is governed by his own temperament, rather than by a style molded through the intellect."

Among the prizes Hennings was awarded were the Walter Lippincott Prize at the Pennsylvania Academy of the Fine Arts in 1925, and in 1926 the Ranger Purchase Award and Isidor Gold Medal at the National Academy of Design, in 1929 first prize of $3000 in the Wild Flowers of Texas competition, and in 1938 first prize at the Academy of Western Painters, Los Angeles.

Although Hennings became a permanent resident of Taos in 1921 and joined the Taos Society of Artists the same year, he retained his Chicago studio from 1917 until the Depression, subletting it for the nine months he spent in Taos and occupying it for the three months he spent in the Windy City to enter exhibitions and attend to business matters. He usually went north late spring until July.

In 1925 Hennings was invited to have a one-man show at Marshall Field and Company in Chicago. Helen Otte, their assistant art director, admired his work—and Hennings admired her. Not only was she a most attractive, gracious young woman, she was also blessed with an independent nature and a taste for adventure. They dated and corresponded for a year before their marriage on July 20, 1926.

For the first 16 months of their marriage, they were in Europe on an extensive painting honeymoon. They bought a Ford touring car for their travels and stayed for five months in France, partly in Nice, right on the Riviera. While her husband Martin painted, Helen Hennings prepared their lunch over sterno. Their life was like a long picnic. Five months in Italy were followed by five more months in Spain before they crossed over to Spanish Morocco for another month. Small portraits and scenes from this long trip are as fresh today as if they were newly painted.

Hennings applied his oils thinly in a sheer layering of strokes. He left his paintings to dry for long periods before applying any varnish, and then he did so with a careful restraint. There is no cracking or yellowing in his work. Craftsmanship was one of the factors that all the early artists of Taos had in common. They knew how to use proven and expert techniques.

When the time came to come home, Hennings took his bride to Taos. Of Taos, Helen Hennings has said, "I was fascinated. I loved Taos right away."

Their home for the next eight years was a small apartment on the grounds of the Harwood Foundation. The studio was in a separate room. Their water pump was also in a separate room. Heating and cooking were done in stoves fueled with either coal or wood, and the ashes had to be hauled each day. Lighting was by kerosene and gasoline lamps. Other facilities, such as the privy, were reached by going outdoors. It was a far cry from city life in Chicago, but it had its own little garden and patio and considerable charm. At that time, Mrs. Burt Harwood still lived in the main house. Today the building is a cultural center in Taos run by the University of New Mexico.

The Waterhole. *Oil, 20 x 24" (51 x 61 cm). McAdoo Galleries, Inc., Woodrow Wilson Fine Arts, Santa Fe.*

THE HENNINGS LIVED a convivial life, yet it was also rather formal. Artists critiqued for each other and they used to gather at their table in the old Columbia Hotel (now the La Fonda Hotel) to talk art, but the wives did not join them. Berninghaus and Ufer, both living as bachelors, frequently used to drop over in the evening for a meal and conversation.

Mary Greene Blumenschein had met Helen Hennings at the Knoedler Gallery in New York when that gallery held a show for Hennings. When the couple arrived in Taos, she gave a reception for them and soon became a warm friend. The Blumenschein home was just a few doors from the Harwood Foundation.

Helen Hennings had been a career woman in the art gallery business. After their marriage, she continued to use her skill as business manager for her husband's career. He was less interested in the business aspects of art and much preferred to spend his days painting. His aspirations were always centered on goals, standards of excellence. "We must do finer work," he once said to his wife. The couple shared everything, and their marriage thrived as a true partnership.

In 1930 the Hennings were expecting a child. On their doctor's advice they drove to Santa Fe in their Model-T Ford along the corrugated roads a full six weeks before the October birth of their daughter. They moved into a temporary apartment across the street from the hospital and Hennings painted in Santa Fe until he could safely take his little family home again. Such expensive precautions were necessary then because there was no hospital in Taos, and travel to Santa Fe was arduous.

In 1936 the Hennings bought a two-story adobe home set on a large plot of what has become a parklike grove of trees on Raton Road. (A willow on the property has recently been judged to have the second largest girth of any such tree in America.) Hennings had a detached studio behind their house. From their windows, the peaks of the Taos mountains loomed up as a backdrop to their private forest.

Hennings was fond of painting in Hondo Canyon during the colorful autumn months. He drove out in the morning, sometimes with his model Frank Zamora, and painted on location most of the day. He usually outstayed other artists such as Bert Phillips, who also enjoyed painting there. Hondo Canyon is several miles north of Taos and is now considered part of the ski area.

Helen Hennings also gives us a glimpse of the closeness of life in Taos in her memory of one painting excursion that could have had a tragic ending: "One day a storm came up. It was nearly six o'clock and Mr. Hennings wasn't down yet. I called Mr. Phillips and told him, 'Martin hasn't returned and I'm worried,' and he said, 'If he doesn't return soon we'll send the posse after him.'

"Well, I was so worried I went next door to ask an artist staying there to drive me out to look for Martin. Just as we got to the fork at the corner down there where the road branches off to Arroyo Seco we saw Martin in a car coming toward us and he recognized us. He had been caught in the storm and had to walk his way out to the head of the canyon where a party who was just leaving gave him a ride. Next day he went out with a mechanic to check on his car and it was covered with snow."

When Helen once asked him why he painted outdoors so late in the afternoon, Hennings told her it was because things would change. He felt an urgency to catch all he could of the subject on location in order to finish it in his studio during the winter. Waterways might change course from one season to the other; trees would look different in different lighting and their branches would take on varied shapes. Each scene had its special beauty. Once Hennings had decided to paint it, he was driven to finish it.

IN THE LATE '30s and early '40s while their daughter was in elementary school, the Hennings spent the second semester in an apartment in Houston, Texas. There he did portraits on commission and also showed his work in an exhibition held by the Sartor Gallery. Portraits always provided a steady part of the family income and Hennings had a gift for capturing the spirit of a person. Among his finest portraits are those of his own two Helens, illustrated in this chapter.

Frank Zamora, a Taos Indian, posed for Hennings for 35 years, usually in the mornings, and helped Helen Hennings with the gardening in the afternoons. They had one of Taos' most notable flower gardens in the patio between the house and the studio. Mrs. Kibbey Couse came to call with sample plants from her garden to share with Helen Hennings in her new home.

Oscar Mayer bought a small portrait head of Frank Zamora and had it on display in his Chicago home. Many prominent visitors frequented the Mayer home and when someone admired the portrait, Mayer impulsively gave it to him. Then he notified Hennings that he wanted "another picture of Frank." All told this happened seven times. Hennings applied himself to making each portrait a work of art distinct from the others. These seven paintings, gathered together, would document the Indian's age over several years. Zamora was killed in an automobile accident some time after Hennings' death.

Robert Rankin White, Hennings' biographer and collector, has cataloged the artist's graphic work, which consisted of eight lithographs and four recently discovered etchings on copper plates. In 1924 and 1925 Hennings drew images on zinc plates for lithographs later pulled at the John and Ollier Lithographic Company in Chicago where the art director was his brother-in-law, Joseph E. Yell. He issued his lithographs in two versions, one in black ink and a smaller number in sepia. They were sold from 1928 until the 1970s. White relates that the price per lithograph at Hennings' death was $15 but rose to as high as $500. Frank Zamora was the model for *Taos Indian;* other titles were *Indian Maiden, Across the Sage, The Frozen Stream, Through Sage and Cedar, Beneath the Cottonwoods, Indian Bake Ovens,* and *The Hunters.*

When the four etching plates were discovered among Hennings' things in 1976, White arranged to have proofs taken. The lithographs and etchings were exhibited in January 1979 at the Museum of Fine Arts in Santa Fe, New Mexico. Robert Rankin White wrote "The Life of E. Martin Hennings, 1886-1956" for the Fall 1978 issue of *El Palacio,* the museum quarterly. His article adds greatly to the available literature on the Taos Society of Artists.

The Depression and war years, with their gas rationing, severely curtailed the market for Taos artists; yet they survived. The WPA with its stipends and mural commissions, was a great help during this stressful period. Hennings painted a pioneer scene as a mural for the Van Buren, Arkansas post office, using his wife and daughter as models.

Slowly things picked up. The Hennings were able to send their daughter to high school at the Loretto Academy in Santa Fe and on to Colorado Springs College. They continued their seasonal trips down into Texas for portrait commissions. He was represented by Jane Hiatt, whose gallery at the La Fonda Hotel was among the best, the first, and the most enduring of the galleries in Taos. Hennings' work sold well and he received a number of commissions.

Across the Sage. *Lithograph, 8 x 9" (20 x 23 cm). Collection Richard and Irma Schuler.*

Beneath the Cottonwoods. *Lithograph, 10 x 10" (25 x 25 cm). Collection Mrs. E.M. Hennings.*

THE FIRST HEART ATTACK hit Hennings in 1954 and it was a warning that all was not well. Nonetheless, he accepted a fine commission from the Santa Fe Railway to do a group of paintings on the Navajo reservation for later use on calendars. The Hennings drove to Ganado in the warm fall of 1955. (Ganado is an important community on the Navajo reservation because of its hospital and high school.) There they rented a furnished hogan from the famous Hubbell Trading Post and established a temporary home for six weeks. A *hogan* is a traditional octagonal structure made of logs patched with adobe. In it there was a bed, a gas cookplate, and a box cooler outside the window. They bought supplies in Gallup once a week and filled in with things from a grocery store in the settlement.

A Swiss nurse at the hospital, hearing that the Hennings were there, introduced herself and with great enthusiasm taught them how to get acquainted with the Navajo people. She advised them first to drop by and visit with a family for a while. Then, she said, they should return the next day with candy for the children and visit again. After getting to know a family, they could ask if they would be willing to pose.

This is just what they did. One older couple posed in shifts. The man posed in the morning as the woman watched the sheep, and then they changed roles in the afternoons. A younger relative was so impressed with the work that he wanted his portrait done, too.

Later, Hennings painted a young mother and her baby, who had fallen asleep on his cradle board. When the family gathered around to see the finished work, they were filled with consternation because they thought the child looked dead. So the artist painted in the baby's eyes as if he were wide awake, and the episode ended happily.

After returning to Taos, Hennings completed his paintings for the railroad. One of them is of a silversmith in a red velvet shirt, kneeling over his task. It has been reproduced widely on a memorial plate.

The Hennings had shared their last painting trip. Soon after the work was finished, Martin Hennings was felled by a second heart attack in May 1956. He is buried in the family plot in Chicago.

Helen Hennings remained in their home under the trees until 1979 when she left Taos, and she has continued to serve her husband's career as she had done for the 30 years of their marriage. With courteous attention she has responded to patrons, scholars, and interested writers, providing them with her time and the help they have requested.

She described her slender, good-looking husband as having been a shy man, an introvert who never joined in disturbances. He devoted himself to his work passionately, in good times and bad, and painted works of lasting beauty with superior craftsmanship. Listening to her cherished memories, you know that theirs had been a love story, and was one still.

Watching the Ceremony. *Etching, 8 x 10" (20 x 25 cm). Collection Robert and Judith White.*

KENNETH MILLER ADAMS
Cubism and Candor

Kenneth M. Adams self-portrait, from catalog of Western Art Gallery, Albuquerque.

KENNETH MILLER ADAMS taught for many years in the art department of the University of New Mexico. He was an excellent, dedicated teacher who served his students at every meeting of the class. He moved without hurry from easel to easel, speaking of specific problems and showing what he meant with sketches or a paintbrush. He provided seasoned solutions to aspiring painters without bruising their egos, and reserved his impatience only for those who lacked sincerity.

Adams was a comfortable-looking man who favored a plaid shirt and baggy pants, slung low; but there was a well-barbered, trimly-mustached gentleman self visible alongside his casual friendly Kansan personality. Adams spoke softly and smiled easily from behind his glasses. His manners were courtly in a most natural way. He projected mastery at the easel, but with such modesty about his own career that you had to make inquiries in order to discover his impressive credits.

Adams was born in Topeka, Kansas, on August 6, 1897 to parents in comfortable circumstances. After an art education that included notable art schools in the States and European academic training as well, he became the last and the youngest member of the Taos Society of Artists, joining the group in 1927, in his 30th year.

At 16, Adams began art studies with George M. Stone, a Topeka artist. Three years later he enrolled in the Art Institute of Chicago and had completed two years of instruction before he was drafted. World War I ended shortly and upon release from the army, he went to New York. There he entered the Art Students League and studied with George B. Bridgeman, Kenneth Hayes Miller, Maurice Sterne, and Eugene Speicher, all venerable teachers in their own way.

The greatest influence on his style and development, though, was Andrew Dasburg, with whom he studied during the summers of 1919 and 1920 at Woodstock, New York. It was Dasburg who introduced Adams to Cézanne's work and to the inventions made by Picasso and the Cubists. Das-

burg's teaching was touched by the zeal of an enthusiast and it struck a sympathetic chord in Adams, so much so that Adams responded to Dasburg before they had ever met. After he saw a Dasburg drawing of a nude on display at the League in New York, he sought out the artist and enrolled in his figure-drawing class, held outdoors in the Woodstock Summer School under the auspices of the League.

In 1921 Adams made his own pilgrimage to France and Italy for further study and painting, six months of which were spent on life drawing. With two friends, Ward Lockwood and Alexander Warshawsky, he spent several months painting landscapes in the south of France. Some of these early scenes, no longer stretched or framed, were found in the Adams estate after his death. They had a muted color scheme which he eventually abandoned in New Mexico, but there was a blocked-out sense of form in them that was a harbinger of his later development. These landscapes were exhibited in Kansas and Missouri after his return to the States in 1923.

It is said that Kenneth Adams followed Andrew Dasburg to New Mexico. He visited him in Santa Fe, but there was no adequate studio space available at the time. So with a letter of introduction from Dasburg to Walter Ufer, Adams moved on to Taos. With Ufer's cordial help, Adams settled right next door on Pueblo Road and became acquainted with the other Taos artists.

Mrs. E. Martin Hennings recalled that Adams made a fairly long trip to Europe after his first stay in Taos. But in 1927 he set up a studio and home next door to the Harwood Foundation on Ledoux Street. The next summer, after his marriage to Hilda Braun Boulton, the newlyweds moved temporarily into the Harwood Foundation, where they had an apartment and studio. In 1930 they moved again to an old adobe house south of Taos, set in the valley near to Spanish farms. Hilda Adams was a helpmate to her husband and helped show his work. Their marriage was close and affectionate.

Harvesters. *Lithograph, 9 x 11 (23 x 28 cm). Collection Mrs. J.R. Modrall.*

TAOS AFFECTED Adams' vision profoundly. More than the other pioneer artists, Adams responded to the Spanish people of the area. He was inspired by respect for their culture. Their seasonal, rural rituals of working in the irrigation ditches, planting, harvesting, and plastering their adobe homes fascinated him. He did portraits of both Indian and Spanish faces. There are lithographs of workers whose solid grace of gesture is the heritage of generations, passed along by rhythmic repetition, year in and year out. Adams portrayed them with monumentality. In the simplicity of their forms, there is a kinship with the Mexican muralist tradition of Orozco, Rivera, and Siquieros, whom Adams much admired. In later years Adams, too, became an experienced muralist. The northern New Mexico landscape also had its place in his work; among his best compositions are those reduced to essentials of form and limited in palette.

Adams' approach to a model was one of unsentimental truth-seeking, but his choice of models reveals his intense interest in their humble dignity. There are unforgettable faces painted by Adams. A suggestion of Cubism is seen in the faceted shapes within shapes. The Adams style matured in Taos. It was here that he wove his own combination of influences together with his taste and sensitivities, to create a mode in the middleground between the academicism of the early Taos founders and the abstraction that stemmed from Cézanne and the Post-Impressionists.

Lloyd Lozés Goff, who wrote a piece about Adams in *New Mexico Artists*, addressed this betwixt-and-between place Adams carved out for himself: "Adams' work combines abstraction and representation, but beside the decorative pastiche of non-objective pictures a painting by Adams looks more representational than abstract. Actually, abstraction figures prominently in his plan, but without any intention to shock or provoke."

Goff goes on to describe Adams' approach to his craft as an outgrowth of his nature: "There are so many fascinating contrivances occupying painters today that the list would be too long to cite here, but Adams uses none; he simply paints. Because he paints in a businesslike manner, never capitalizing on 'fortunate' mistakes, his paintings show deliberate analysis. The action they contain is abstracted from real movement and is based upon linear and spatial concepts, not necessarily upon actuality. Adams frequently uses and re-uses the same subject, exploring its possibilities in lithography, oil, and watercolor over a period of years.

"The inability of critics to classify Adams' work is the least of his concerns. The academic critic has called his work, derogatively, 'abstract,' while the 'modernist,' just as derogatively, has called it 'academic.' The latter complains because his forms are recognizable, and the former because his forms are not three-dimensional but two-dimensional!"

Adams was a man's man. He loved fishing in the streams that abound in the Taos mountains. One of his fishing pals was the prominent Albuquerque lawyer, Dick Modrall, who wrote about Adams in a fine catalog published by the Western Art Gallery in 1972:

"Early in my acquaintance and friendship with him, I imagined that he combined two skills which should complement each other perfectly. I could imagine an artist like Ken going into our northern New Mexico mountains in the fall when the aspen and oak brush coloring was at its height and trout fishing at its best, fishing a good stream for a couple of hours, then setting up his easel or sketch board and sketching or painting during midday, then returning to his fly fishing in the latter part of the afternoon. After a few trips together when never a sign of a sketch pad, pencil, easel, or paint brush appeared, I asked him if he never combined his painting and sketching with his fishing. He replied that he had long since learned that the two were wholly incompatible .... He always concentrated on one or the other."

Photo Jonathan A. Meyers

Francesca. *Lithograph, 16 x 12" (41 x 31 cm). Collection Mrs. J.R. Modrall.*

Taos Indian Woman. *Lithograph, 9 x 12" (23 x 31 cm). Collection The Edwin B. Nelsons.*

Nude. *Conté charcoal, 20 x 28" (51 x 71 cm). Collection Mrs. J.R. Modrall.*

Nude. *Charcoal, 19 x 12½" (48 x 32 cm). Collection The Edwin B. Nelsons.*

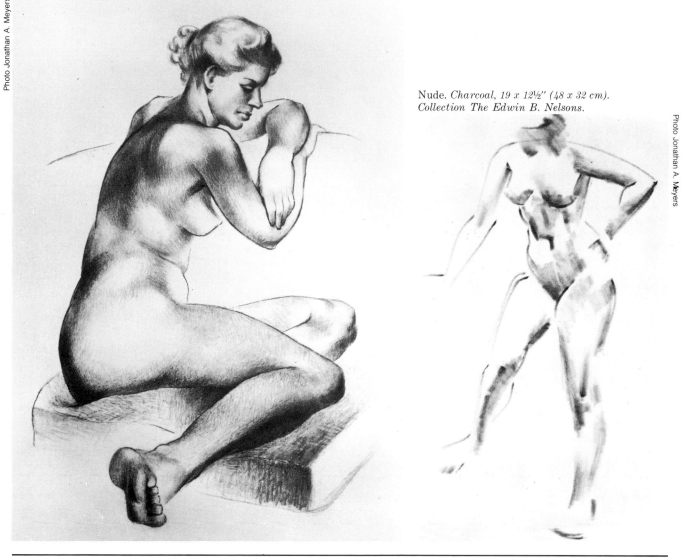

IT WAS DURING his 14 years in Taos that Adams began his teaching career. After the Harwood Foundation became the site of the University of New Mexico Field School of Art in 1929, Adams taught there each summer. In 1933 he taught the fall term in Albuquerque. This, followed by his enrollment in a governmental program that paid artists to paint, was a boost to his finances. The regional director of this program was the Santa Fe painter and printmaker Gustave Baumann. He selected Adams for the highest available salary under the Treasury Department guidelines: $42.50 per week. This was the poor period for all the Taos artists, just as it was for most everyone, and it was a lucky break for Adams to have such security. He painted murals as his part of the project: one for the post office at Goodland, Kansas, called *Rural Free Delivery* that was reproduced in *Time* magazine, (March 2, 1936), and another for the post office at Deming, New Mexico.

In 1938 Adams was elected an Associate of the National Academy of Design. That year he moved to Albuquerque as "artist-in-residence" at the University of New Mexico on a grant from the Carnegie Foundation for two years. In 1940 he was appointed head of the art department at the Sandia School, a private girls' academy in Albuquerque. He also taught part-time at the university.

Hilda Adams was in frail health with tuberculosis, and until her death in 1948, much of the decade was taken up with caring for his wife and fulfilling his teaching duties. Goff has said that Adams did not enjoy teaching at first, but came to love it.

In 1949 Adams married Helen Osborn Hogrefe and thereby gained a son, Larry Hogrefe, and happiness. For three years, 1950, 1951, and 1952 he directed the Field School of Art in Taos for the university. The people of the Taos Valley, both the Indians and the Spanish farmers, became the subjects of new work.

Larry was a youngster in high school then and he recalls his own fish stories and the companionship he had with his stepfather. They drove up to the Hondo Canyon north of Taos occasionally and if the water in the river was muddy, Adams would paint watercolors, but if it was clear, he fished. They shared fishing trips into the Rio Grande Canyon, looking for the big fish that came out of the river into the deep pools of the creeks.

During the long summer twilights in Taos, after the Field School classes at the Harwood Foundation were over for the day, Larry and Adams joined their next-door neighbor Emil Bisttram, who took them fishing in his jeep into places they could not have gotten to otherwise.

Television was new in the early '50s, and Adams became a devoted fan of football and baseball through their Albuquerque neighbor's set. After the Adams got their own television set, he would sit with Larry's toy bulldog on his lap, engrossed in the game. His love of sports extended to giving a helping hand once in a while to a university athlete who signed up for one of his classes.

The business side of art was not Adams' interest and he sometimes expressed surprise when people wanted to buy his work. After their marriage, Helen Adams helped manage the details of his career, such as getting his work to shows on time and contacting his patrons.

N THE NARROWER CONFINES of city life in Albuquerque, Adams turned increasingly to his garden. He grew flowers enthusiastically, among them iris, zinnias, roses, and Iceland poppies. When he was able to raise the poppies successfully from seeds, he shared the plants with his friends. He had favorite vases for different flowers and he observed that the blossoms seemed to grow larger sometimes after they were brought indoors and arranged.

Adams' flower paintings are mature work and in them his mastery of color is clear. He drew and modeled wth his brush simultaneously. To give roundness, he relied on the contrast of warm and cool as he applied strokes in a subtle but simplified sequence of colors. Each stroke retains its identity and is placed confidently.

In the flower paintings, his color is brilliant and in some areas is laid down with transparency. There is a fully realized form and texture in the flowers and there is an elusive quality about them of delight. Both the painter and the gardener were enchanted by the vibrant, healthy bouquets. The somber note usually felt in his human subjects is missing from the florals.

What distinguishes Adams from the other Taos artists is a body of work reflecting his lifelong study of the nude. He was a devoted and patient practitioner of drawing from life. The drawings are quite varied, not only in media but in purpose. Some are pencil and some watercolor, but most are Conté or charcoal. In some he rendered form in line and value with classic, academic prowess. In others he reduced form to basic cubistic shapes, but not rigidly or by formula. Still others are portraits, and some are featureless torsos. His preoccupation was the creation of form in space—not storytelling or visual description of detail.

Adams painted nudes and taught painting from life in oil. His lessons on turning a nose by a gradation from warm to cool shades were superb, especially when he demonstrated it with his brush. He could also render the hand in shading with remarkable dexterity. But the real enjoyment for him was in the pigment and chromatic relationships.

Goff wrote that "Adams holds to his own disposition for candor." This interesting remark opens a line of thought about the artist. His candor, his lack of artiness or contrivance, has its mysteries. With his apparent straight-forwardness he simply painted, as Goff said, workers, ethnic portraits, nudes and florals, but he connected with them on different emotional levels. Flowers gave him joy. Those who toiled gained his respect; it was his intellectual tendency to portray them as symbols of "Man, the Worker." The nudes, over and over again, were solidly three-dimensional, in varied classic poses. Adams' nudes are so sculptural that you wonder that he was not also a modeler in clay. However, they are almost without sensuality. Adams, the observer, dominated the work. He rarely reveals an emotional response to the nude. There is far more emotion in his paintings of the Spanish villagers of Taos.

In 1961 the National Academy of Design elected Adams to full membership as an Academician. He remained on the faculty of the University of New Mexico as an important member of the art department until 1963. In 1964, the university held a retrospective in the Museum of Art, accompanied by an excellent catalog.

Kenneth Adams died in 1966 in Albuquerque. After his death, his widow Helen helped prepare a major show of the work in his estate. It was held by the Western Gallery of Art after Helen Adams' death in 1972. An award-winning catalog, edited by Ruth Dick, was published in conjunction with the show.

Taos Indian. *Charcoal drawing, 14 x 16" (36 x 41 cm). Collection Mrs. J.R. Modrall.*

The Plasterers. *Lithograph, 11½ x 14¾" (29 x 37 cm). Collection Mrs. J.R. Modrall.*

Taos Hoop Dancer. *Oil, 30 x 30'' (76 x 76 cm). Private collection.*

The Taos Farmers. *Oil, 40¼ x 36¼" (102 x 92 cm). The San Antonio Art League.*

'Interrieur. Oil, 36 x 24" (91 x 61 cm), Collection Mr. and Mrs. Toy Dixon Savage, Jr.

Portrait of Mrs. E. Martin Hennings. *Oil, 24 x 20' (61 x 51 cm). Collection Mrs. E.M. Hennings.*

Portrait of the Berber. *Oil, 14 x 14″ (36 x 36 cm). Collection Mrs. E.M. Hennings.*

The Victor. Oil, 48 x 52" (122 x 132 cm). Collection Harrison Eiteljorg.

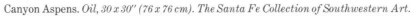

Canyon Aspens. *Oil, 30 x 30" (76 x 76 cm). The Santa Fe Collection of Southwestern Art.*

Taos Valley in Winter. *Oil, 12 x 14" (30 x 36 cm). Collection Mrs. E.M. Hennings.*

Portrait of Daughter Helen at 17. *Oil, 30 x 36" (76 x 91 cm). Collection Mrs. E.M. Hennings.*

Through Sunlit Aspens. *Oil, 30 x 36″ (76 x 91 cm). Private collection.*

Photo Jonathan A. Meyers

Thistle Blossoms. *Oil, 36½ x 36½″ (93 x 93 cm). Won Edgar B. Davis prize of $3000 in 1928 for best Texas wildflower painting. Collection Museum of Fine Arts, Museum of New Mexico, Santa Fe. On permanent loan from Mrs. Edgar Tobin.*

Iceland Poppies. *Oil, 20 x 24" (51 x 61 cm). Collection Mrs. J.R. Modrall.*

Iris. Oil, 14 x 18" (36 x 46 cm). Collection Mrs. J.R. Modrall.

The Dry Ditch, *1964. Oil, 50 x 36" (127 x 91 cm).*
Collection Harrison Eiteljorg.

Early French Landscape. *Oil, 20 x 26" (51 x 66 cm). McAdoo Galleries Inc., Woodrow Wilson Fine Arts, Santa Fe.*

Flamingo Iris. *Oil, 24 x 18″ (61 x 46 cm). McAdoo Galleries Inc., Woodrow Wilson Fine Arts, Santa Fe.*

SOME WHO FOLLOWED

LEON GASPARD, The Bridge Pesquashik.
Oil, 24 x 36" (61 x 91 cm).
Collection Harrison Eiteljorg

Andrew Dasburg

Autumn Fruit. *Oil (?), 23 x 29" (58 x 74 cm). Collection the Harwood Foundation, University of New Mexico, Taos.*

WHEN HE ARRIVED in 1918, Andrew Dasburg brought the Post-Impressionist discoveries of Cézanne and Picasso to New Mexico.

Though born in Paris in 1887, Dasburg was raised in the Hell's Kitchen section of New York by his widowed immigrant mother, who supported him as a seamstress of stage costumes. A childhood accident lamed him for life—and added glamour to his fragile, blond good looks.

In 1902 Dasburg began studying art with Kenyon Cox and Frank V. DuMond at the Art Students League. He took night classes in life drawing with George Bridgman and summer landscape classes under Birge Harrison at Woodstock, New York. In 1907 he studied in the night classes of Robert Henri.

On a trip to France in 1909-1910, Dasburg met the inner circle of Paris salon life—the Steins, Picasso, Matisse, and most importantly, Ambroise Vollard, the dealer of work by Paul Cézanne, who had died only three years before. Dasburg said of Cézanne's paintings, "Reality was there" (Asha Briesen, *The Taos News*.) He studied Cézanne's work zealously. For a time he borrowed a long, horizontal still life by Cézanne of apples, owned by the Steins, and copied it many times to better understand its formal geometry.

By the time Dasburg returned to New York, his future path was already marked dand his effect on American artists was immediately felt. Dasburg became a teacher at Woodstock and a vital member of the embryonic New York avant-garde. In 1913 he and his first wife, the sculptor Grace Mott Johnson (he always called her "Johnson"), were both represented in the Armory Show, probably the most important event in the history of American contemporary art of this century. Dasburg's entries were a landscape, two still lifes, and a Cubist plaster carving of Lucifer, greatly influenced by Matisse.

Dasburg was always an experimental artist. Before a second trip to France in 1914, he produced five abstract improvisations associated with the birth of Synchronism. These paintings were his only totally nonobjective works, and they have a legend of their own.

He took one of them to Mabel Dodge's home on Fifth Avenue after being invited to her salon. She was away, but the stage designer Robert (Bobby) Edmond Jones was holding the fort for her and he suggested they hang the painting in her house with the name on it *The Absence of Mabel*, which she enjoyed on her return. He then painted two more abstractions and called them *To Mabel Dodge Number One* and *To Mabel Dodge Number Two*. One of these was given the title *The Presence of Mabel*. For a time they were given sarcastic coverage—fruitful attention as it turned out—by critics.

After her move to Taos with the artist Maurice Sterne, who was her husband at the time, Mabel Dodge invited Dasburg to visit them. He (and later, at his urging, Johnson with their son Alfred) made a visit to the village in the winter of 1918. He was immediately enthused about the dramatic landscape of the area.

HROUGH ALL THE ROMANTIC vicissitudes of his life thereafter, New Mexico was his home. He moved permanently to Taos in 1932 and he established his home and studio in old adobe buildings south of the town in the village of Talpa. In this austere setting, bare of anything but necessities, Dasburg continued his long career. From 1937 to 1947 Addison's disease almost destroyed him, but with the advent of new drugs, he regained his place in art and continued his development as an experimental artist. The process of his evolution was always toward greater synthesis and further reduction of elements. His favorite subject matter was drawn from the vistas of Taos Valley—the mountains, clouds, adobe houses, and fields. His other subjects were close in spirit to those of Cézanne—still lifes with fruit, flowers, portraits, and trees by the road.

Dasburg usually spent his mornings drawing from nature. From his observations he selected, with extreme sensitivity, those lines of force within the natural scene which he alone seemed to perceive and from them he created precisely balanced compositions. With diagonals, he introduced tension. With verticals and horizontals, he provided repose. His effort was to maintain a delicate poise between the two emotions. For Dasburg there was a relationship between the lines and colors of the artist's repertoire and the elements used by a composer to create music.

Through oil, pastel, ink, watercolor, and, in his late eighties, lithographs, Dasburg always found a way to apply his private geometry to the world he inhabited.

He also found a way to share his findings with other artists. Jerry Bywaters wrote in *The Arts*, July 1924 (requoted in a 1959 catalog): "Dasburg himself, always in the vanguard of things, had much to say as a teacher and writer, including these introductory remarks on Cubism: 'Cubism is a geometry of rhythm and an architecture of matter. Two considerations are fundamental to the understanding of rhythm. One is the force of gravity, the other the upward impulse in living things. All matter shows the effect of one or both of these conditions, and they are two important factors in the invisible moulding of all forms.'"

Dasburg's ideas had their impact on many artists whom he outlived. Kenneth Adams moved to New Mexico because Dasburg was there. J. Ward Lockwood, also a former pupil of Dasburg's at Woodstock, followed Adams to Taos. Cady Wells was inspired by Dasburg's vision to discover his own abstractions in the landscape of New Mexico, as were Tony Mygatt and Earl Stroh. Victor Higgins, who ignored the ferment of invention while studying in Europe, nonetheless found in the Cubist planes and rhythms of Dasburg's work a new direction for himself. Howard Cook has given credit to Dasburg for bringing new currents of thought to the Southwest from which he and others benefited, including Cook's wife Barbara Latham.

Dasburg occupies a singular position as an artist of great versatility and influence who stood apart from the Taos Society of Artists and brought new interpretations to the valley as distinctive and lasting as those of the pioneers. Dasburg died peacefully on August 13, 1979 at his home in Talpa.

Andrew Dasburg.

Howard N. Cook and Barbara Latham

HOWARD N. COOK was born in Springfield, Massachusetts in 1901 and spent a lot of time on his grandfather's farm in Greenfield. He spent three sessions at the Art Students League in New York where he studied life drawing under George Bridgman; and for a short while was in an experimental class with Andrew Dasburg, Max Weber, and others who imparted the modern trends in Europe enthusiastically to their students.

Cook recalls, "I was a green young thing. It was my first year at the League. It was over my head at that time. Later, looking back, it was terrific, Dasburg made me aware of trends that I studied for myself when I went to France."

From 1922 to 1927 Cook worked as an illustrator for top magazines such as *Forum* and *Century*. In 1926 *Forum* ran Willa Cather's *Death Comes to the Archbishop* in serial form. They commissioned Cook to do a series of woodcuts and etchings of the New Mexico area, the setting for Cather's book, to be featured in the same issue. Cook lived for two months in Santa Fe before moving to an old, small hotel in Taos. At a dance he met fellow-artist Barbara Latham and they were married in 1927 in Santa Fe. They traveled for eight years before settling in Talpa, a tiny village south of Taos. For a number of years they spent winters in the East and continued their careers from an eastern base.

They went to Paris in 1929 and Cook studied on his own at a famous lithographic workshop while Latham sketched out in the streets. During 1932-1933 the couple lived in Mexico on a Guggenheim Fellowship. It was there that Cook developed his knowledge of fresco painting and found inspiration for a number of murals he later completed. There are Cook murals in the courthouses of Springfield, Massachusetts and Pittsburgh, Pennsylvania. For the latter mural Cook won the annual gold medal given by the Architectural League of New York. In 1937 he began a two-and-a-half-year project to paint murals in the San Antonio, Texas post office. The wall is cut with a number of arches, and Cook accounted for them in his energetic design, which won national competition sponsored by the Section of Fine Arts in Washington, D.C. Cook's technique was a classic one, requiring the treatment of the wall with slake lime and careful preparations. He worked out the composition in detail and in full scale on a continuous roll of paper while still in Taos, then translated it to the wall. His subject, the figures of those who affected the history of San Antonio from the Conquistadors to modern cattlemen, is penetrated with excitement. The mural was the largest government fresco in the United States at that time, 750 square feet of continuous mural.

In 1954 Cook completed a mural on a philosophical theme, *Man's Responsibility to His Fellow Man*, for the Mayo Clinic in Minnesota. The commission took two and a half years to complete.

Cook has been an energetic, growing artist whose work has become increasingly abstract. He acknowledges that he has felt Dasburg's influence on the direction he has followed in his art. As a teacher, he has been an influence himself at the Universities of Texas, California at Berkeley, and New Mexico (in both the summer session at Taos and the regular session in Albuquerque), as well as at the Minneapolis Art Institute.

During World War II Cook was a war artist, landing on beaches right along with the troops in the Solomon Islands. Upon his return in the late summer of 1943, he produced some powerful lithographs of his experiences in rich darks that have the stamp of an eye-witness viewpoint. In 1949 he was elected to membership in the National Academy as a graphic artist.

In the '40s Cook was known for his watercolors, such as his scenes of Taos Valley. In later years he also painted oils of Indian dancers, and landscapes that are filled with texture and abstract decoration, and are more involved with rhythm than pictorial accuracy. To create the effect of a dance, for example, he worked out a schematic design whose pulsating vitality relates to the movement of the dancers. This quality of energy in the work itself links Cook's paintings, murals, and prints throughout the subtle changes in his style. "I've always wanted the suggestion of movement in my work," he says.

Cook, an idealist, spoke with Ernest Watson for an article in *American Artist* (March 1945), and explained his concept of the artist's role: "It is up to the artist to find and instill in his work the secret movements that will reveal life, and he alone can do it with his mental and emotional inventions revealing a synthesis of invaluable results which no mechanical approach can ever equal."

Barbara Latham and Howard Cook, c. 1945.

HOWARD COOK,Winter Mountain Cycle No. 4. *Oil, 26 x 55" (66 x 140 cm).Collection Museum of Fine Arts, Museum of New Mexico, Santa Fe.Gift of Howard Cook.*

BARBARA LATHAM, Camposanto. *Oil, 18" x 24" (46 x 61 cm). Collection Museum of Fine Arts, Museum of New Mexico, Santa Fe.*

BARBARA LATHAM, like her husband Howard Cook, is a tall New England-born artist born in Walpole, Massachusetts, and raised in Connecticut. She had her training at the Art Students League in the summer at Woodstock under Andrew Dasburg, with whom she studied painting from the nude model.

Latham is accomplished in a number of media. There has been a duality in her career from the beginning. She has had many one-artist shows and has been included in important museum exhibitions and collections as an easel painter. But she has also been a notable illustrator of children's books, frequently with animal and insect themes. Some of her books are *Pedro, Niña and Perito*, which is a collector's item now; *The Silver Dollar*; *Tree Frog*; *I Like Butterflies*; and *Flying Horse Shoe Ranch*. Her one adult book was Frank Dobie's *Tales of Old-Time Texas*, which she illustrated with accurate and sometimes humorous pencil drawings.

Barbara Latham arrived in Taos in 1925 and worked on her own prints as well as on designs for Foster's Greeting Card Company in Ranchos de Taos. Foster's had a Sturges Etching Press and for a time was a thriving enterprise.

After their meeting, she and Howard Cook found they had much in common. They had grown up within 50 miles of each other and shared not only a background but also their mutual commitment to art. They had many early adventures traveling the menacing, nearly vacant New Mexico desert as Cook fulfilled his *Forum* assignment. It took them five days of camping to reach the Hopi village of Walpi, driving in an old Chevy coupe that had belonged to Dorothy Brett. Cook gave a funny account of this trip in *Recuerdos/ Early Days of the Blumenschein Family* by Helen Greene Blumenschein.

The Cooks found their Taos home while out horseback riding south of town near the village of Talpa in 1935. "It was a wreck," Latham recalls. They rebuilt the old adobe house up on the hillside and improved it over many years of residence. Their job lay in the panoramic view of Ranchos de Taos valley, which has furnished subject matter for many of Latham's paintings. She has painted it from every view in all seasons. There are her scenes of agricultural life; still lifes of her own vegetables, fruits, and flowers; and the patterns of ceremonial life of their neighbors in the Spanish community.

Patterns play an important part in her work. Tightly packed with forms, her pictures are lively and vibrant with color. She builds an intricate abstract design, linking the pictorial elements together. "I'm especially fond of design and color," she says. "All that subject matter of the villages, both the Spanish and the Indian, lend themselves to my style. Now I'm doing only oils of my memories from Taos in 1925."

Barbara Latham and Howard Cook moved to Santa Fe in 1976.

John Ward Lockwood

J. Ward Lockwood. Courtesy Fenn Galleries, Ltd., Santa Fe.

JOHN WARD LOCKWOOD was born in 1894 in Atchison, Kansas. He had a fine education at the University of Kansas, the Philadelphia Academy of Fine Arts, and the Académie Ransom in Paris. He also studied in Andrew Dasburg's classes at Woodstock, where he met fellow-Kansan Kenneth Adams. In 1926, he followed Adams to Taos, searching for cheap living conditions among colleagues rather than for Indian subject matter. He liked what he found and stayed for some time, living in an adobe home at the Harwood Foundation.

Lockwood's paintings owe something to influences from Cubism via Dasburg and also John Marin, with whom he shared painting and fishing jaunts in 1929 and 1930. His focus on the streets and daily life of the Taos village and the landscapes of the Taos valley led to paintings both pictorial and also sufficiently descriptive to give the viewer a sense of the lifestyle and area at that time, without sentimentality. In a way, his was an "Ash Can" viewpoint of the tiny plaza at Taos.

The pleasure of his work lies in his free rearrangements of form. Storefront, adobe house, horse, mountain, and tree become simplified parts of a canted surface in a contemporary work. Such a description of his art would not appeal to Lockwood himself, however. He once told Ina Sizer Cassidy: "I'm tired of these terms—Modern Art—Conservative Art—Classical Art. There's only one Art. The mode in which it is presented doesn't determine the question. It is either Art or it isn't and that's an end to it" (*New Mexico Magazine*, February 1933).

As it happens, Lockwood's work grew progressively freer of realistic perspective and more involved in designing schematic patterns relating to landscape. His inventiveness with eclectic stimuli made for a varied body of work.

Lockwood did a number of WPA murals: in the Taos County Court House; the Federal Court House of Lexington, Kentucky; post offices in Wichita, Kansas, and Edinburg and Hamilton, Texas; and in the Post Office Department Building, Washington, D.C. He taught lithography for a season at the Broadmoor School of Art in Colorado Springs. Toward the end of the Depression, Lockwood left Taos to establish and head the art department at the University of Texas and to teach at the University of California at Berkeley. He died in 1963.

Exciting Winter Day. *Watercolor, 13⅞ x 19″ (35 x 48 cm). Permanent Collection Roswell Museum and Art Center, Roswell, New Mexico. Gift of Mr. and Mrs. J.L. Hughes.*

Cady Wells

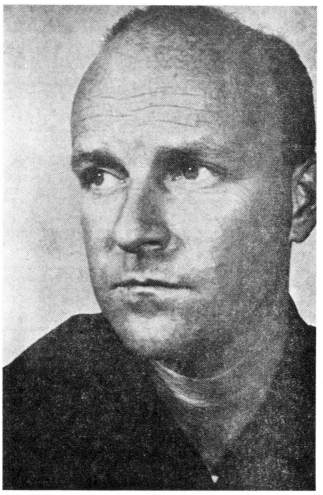

Cady Wells. Photo reproduced from a newspaper clipping.

CADY WELLS was born in Massachusetts in 1904. His family was wealthy and he enjoyed financial independence throughout his relatively short life. Wells was something of a dilettante who studied scenic design, flower arrangement, and brush drawing in Japan, and music—he was a fine pianist. In the summer of 1932 he studied painting in Taos with Andrew Dasburg and found his true métier in which all the various strains of his taste found an outlet.

Wells excelled at watercolor, both transparent and opaque, which he used in bold abstract designs with a musical notation, definitely rhythmic and sophisticated. His landscapes of New Mexico are intelligently conceived but emotionally painted statements. To portray Taos Moun-tain and other subjects, he made patterns of thick and thin black lines that are alive with energy and complex in their relationships.

Wells traveled widely and was respected for his work, which fits into a group of semi-abstract statements by those who knew Dasburg and shared his vision. For them nature furnished thoughts as well as clues to design. Despite the Dasburg influence, Wells was an independent artist.

For a few years Wells lived outside of Santa Fe, filling a role as artist and art patron; but during World War II, he served in the army. In 1952 Wells returned to New Mexico from the Virgin Islands where he went to live in 1949. He died in Santa Fe in 1954 after several heart attacks.

Cady Wells in his studio.

Helen Greene Blumenschein

Self-portrait, *early 1930s. Oil.*

HELEN GREENE BLUMENSCHEIN has been associated with Taos since 1919, when her famous mother, Mary Greene Blumenschein, agreed at last to live in the village that her equally famous father, Ernest L. Blumenschein, so passionately needed.

He picked them up at the Raton station and drove them home in his new Model-T Ford, which had some trouble navigating the Paloflecho Pass. It was the second time the Blumenschein women had come West. In 1913 everything went wrong and Mary had returned to New York with her four-year-old child. This time she came, she was determined to stick it out.

From the first, Helen Blumenschein thrived in this emotionally entangled environment. She went fishing with her father and became an expert angler. At home she was given the freedom to express herself in art in her own way.

Though she had some schooling in Taos, she spent several winters back in New York while her mother studied jewelry-making at Pratt Institute. Exposure to the sophistication of New York as well as to the enclosed multi-cultural society of Taos marks Helen Blumenschein's life. She is a studious and objective observer and recorder of the Taos scene in art and word—and is also a partisan member of that scene who has contributed greatly to its continuity.

She attended Packer Collegiate Institute in Brooklyn Heights, New York through high school, and then went to France. From 1929 to 1931 she studied art in Paris, and then returned to Taos. Each spring for four years she spent two months in New York studying silkscreening and lithography at the Art Students League. Her career was interrupted during World War II, when she served as a First Lieutenant in the WAAC as a censor of Spanish mail in the South Pacific. She came home in 1945 to look after her aging parents.

Helen Blumenschein's work until 1960 included serigraphy and lithography. Her prints received acclaim and invitations for exhibitions, both nationally and internationally.

Her large brush and ink landscapes of New Mexico, although one of a kind, have the strong, graphic qualities of a print with a well-developed sense of pattern. She opposes black and white areas and embellishes both with a personal code of lines, crosshatches, and squiggles that animate and define the surface. She is also known for her portraits in charcoal, some of which were reproduced in her book *Sounds and Sights of Taos Valley.*

In addition to the zealous effort Helen Blumenschein has made to preserve the records of her parents' lives and careers, she has also become an expert in the environs of Taos and has been honored for her work in archaeology and history. She has written and lectured extensively.

A serious woman of commitment, she has a unique way of planning her life in stages, deciding ahead of time that she will pursue a certain goal for a given number of years and then move on to the next preplanned activity. For some time her goal was to complete *Aránzazu,* an account of the history of Taos Valley, based on her research.

Today she is once again working intensely on her art, especially oil painting. She is modest about her considerable achievements and claims that, in her opinion, her best work so far is in her portrait drawings in charcoal and Conté chalk and her inks; so she will devote more time to her oils. Her painting trips take her to many areas of the West and she is often in motion, but Helen Greene Blumenschein continues to spend at least half of the year in her family home in Taos. She has arranged that the home belongs to the Kit Carson Foundation as a gift to the heritage of the town. Her father's studio and the west end of the house, six of the eleven rooms, are now open to the public in the summer.

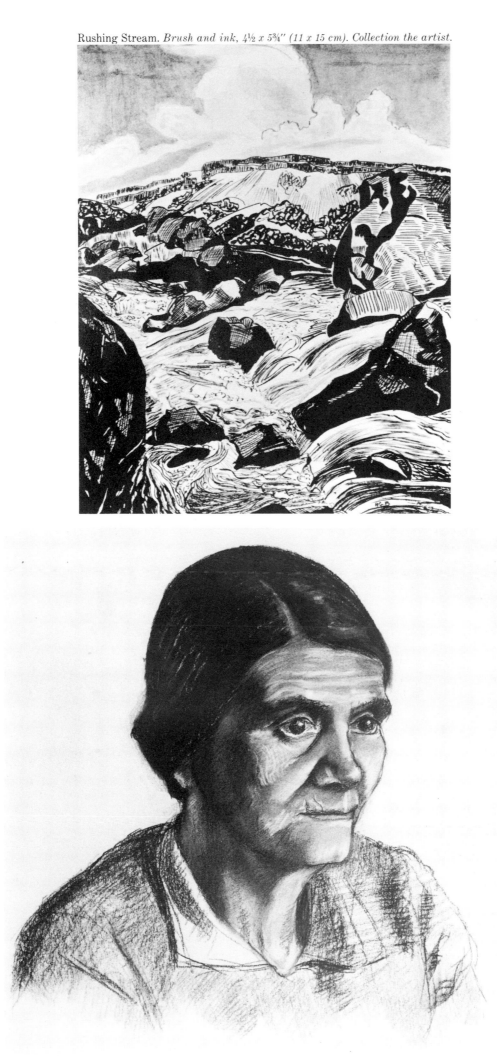

Rushing Stream. *Brush and ink, 4½ x 5¾″ (11 x 15 cm). Collection the artist.*

Emelia. *Conté chalk and charcoal, 19 x 14″ (48 x 36 cm).*
The Harwood Foundation, University of New Mexico, Taos.

Ila McAfee

ILA MCAFEE was born October 21, 1897, on the north side of the Cochetopa Range where her father had a sawmill 20 miles southeast of Gunnison, Colorado, a mining and cattle town.

McAfee recalls, "The sawmill was later moved to the Crested Butte area—a very rugged and beautiful, wild mountain country—and there as a young child I spent the summers in the small streams and forest edges in a wonderful playground.

"My family spend the winters on a small ranch in the Cochetopa valley where the snows were deep in the mountains. Later the sawmill was sold and the ranch was enlarged and became our permanent home. The herd of cattle slowly grew and so domestic animals became company for me and their care taught me the responsibility and work one learns early in country living."

There was always a shepherd dog or two to drive the cattle. Just driving back and forth over the five miles to the country school she attended, McAfee learned something of the habits of wild animals. In the winter she became familiar with their tracks. "We saw four coyotes at once one morning which gave us a thrill. Then there were beaver, marmots, rabbits, prairie dogs, chipmunks and ground squirrels; rarely a deer or antelope. We found elk antlers although there were no elk around then; but now they have been brought back into the northern hills around Gunnison. There were many different birds, including sage hens.

"While growing up I drew horses, not so much from life but from memory and observation. I can draw horses in any position because I know their anatomy and how they look and what they can do. I do horse portraits from life if the horse is around, but my imaginary compositions and all action pictures are painted from imagination or memory and from knowledge of the horse."

McAfee's horses have a vibrant energy, dramatized with tossing manes and tails. Her spontaneous drawing has an Oriental grace and freedom. She expresses any mood, from literal to make-believe, in her paintings. "I paint very rapidly and sometimes start with no preliminary drawing at all; but usually I have the idea and composition worked out beforehand."

Horses by McAfee are widely distributed throughout the world via Walter Foster's *How to Draw Horses*, one of his best sellers. Her painting, *The Four Seasons*, reproduced on the Foster cover is owned by the Stark Museum of Orange, Texas, although reproduction rights belong to Foster. McAfee has also painted 15 portraits of Lutcher Stark's longhorn steers on his private park "Shangra La" and these, plus a painting of a herd of steer, are in his collection.

After graduating from high school in Gunnison, McAfee spent a year at West Lake School of Art and Haz Art School in Los Angeles before enrolling at Western State College, a two-year normal school at that time. She graduated in 1919 and left for Chicago where she studied painting with the muralist James E. McBurney and served as his assistant until 1924. She was a protegé of the sculptor Loredo Taft. "I lived at the Taft Studio along with some other art students, but I did not study with Taft. I did help out several sculptors when there were animals in their sculpture groups."

McAfee studied in New York at the Art Students League and the National Academy of Design in 1925 and 1926. During her two years in the city she illustrated animal stories for magazines and books. She also did portraits of a Morgan mare and an Irish setter for Chauncy F. Stillman.

In 1926 McAfee married Elmer Page Turner, who had been a fellow student of McBurney's. The ceremony was held at her family's ranch and they honeymooned in Taos.

In 1928 the Turners moved permanently to Taos and built The White Horse Studio on Armory Place, two blocks from the plaza. For years her small sculpture of a white horse was atop the fire wall and it was this piece that gave the name to the studio. The horse is a working model, about 20″ (51 cm) high, for a lifesized horse she made in the '30s that was featured at an Orange Show in San Bernardino, California. Recently she brought the carved plaster piece down and almost recreated it. It can be seen in the front window of the studio now where it is protected from the weather.

The White Horse Studio was a productive source of paintings for both Turners. Ila McAfee painted murals at her studio that were later mounted under her instruction in the post offices of Clifton, Texas; Cordell and Edmund, Oklahoma; and Gunnison, Colorado. The latter mural, entitled *Wealth of the West* is a scene of a cattle drive. There is a rancher, prospector, and a fisherman in the mural as well.

As a tribute to her mother-in-law, Edith Turner, McAfee presented three murals—*Buffalo, Deer,* and *Antelope*—to the public library of Greeley, Colorado where Mrs. Turner had served as assistant librarian for many years.

In addition to her easel paintings, which number nearly 1000, McAfee has designed fabrics, wrapping paper, dishes, and calendars. Sculpture and woodcarving also have had a continuing place in her work.

McAfee's work can be seen at the Stables Gallery, Taos Inn, Kachina Lodge, and in her studio, which is open to the public. In the half century of her career in Taos, McAfee has received numerous honors. Among them are every award given by the New Mexico State Fair Professional Juried Show: first, second, third, fourth, Grand Prize, and Purchase Prize, in addition to the Popular Vote. Ila McAfee has truly centered her career in the Southwest, especially in her adopted state of New Mexico.

Longhorns on the Range. *Oil, 25½ x 43¾″ (65 x 111 cm). Purchase prize winner, New Mexico State Fair, Permanent Collection.*

White Horse. *Modeling plaster, 22½ x 25½″ (57 x 65 cm).*
Collection Ila McAfee.

Moonlight Madness. *Oil, 28″ x 22″ (71 x 56 cm). Collection Dr. Esther Van Pelt.*

141

Gene Kloss

Gene Kloss in her studio.

WHEN GENE KLOSS and her husband, poet-composer Phillips Kloss, made a camping honeymoon trip to Taos in 1925, an unusual passenger in their convertible car was her 60-pound etching press. Gene Kloss is a westerner. She was born in Oakland, California, in 1903. She was graduated with honors from the University of California at Berkeley in 1924 and did further work at the California School of Fine Arts in San Francisco and the College of Arts and Crafts in Oakland.

From 1925 until the '40s, the Klosses lived in Taos in the warm weather and spent winters in Berkeley. Her reputation was established on the West Coast in the '20s and '30s when she had many one-woman shows of paintings and etchings in San Francisco and elsewhere. Her reputation spread through her participation in group shows across the nation, resulting in frequent praise from critics.

In Taos she responded to the landscape of mountains and plains, snow and sun, and to the architecture of the Indians and Spanish. She witnessed the ceremonies of both groups and reacted with a sensitive empathy reached after patient hours of observation.

To make prints reflecting the tonal richness of these subjects, Kloss turned to aquatint. She relied on herself and E. S. Lumsden's classic book *The Art of Etching* for education in technique.

The distinctive Kloss style in etching, drypoint and aquatint, watercolor, and oil is graceful and organized, very much like the artist herself. Kloss has created many figurative prints, often in a combination of etching techniques, with deft value control. Her effort is to present her theme as an arresting formal composition of abstract elements underscored by an intuitive spiritual quality. From long association with the Taos Indians, she has absorbed and shares their reverence for nature. Her prints of Indian dancers give the effect of activity. With line and value she creates a rhythm that repeats the musical beat or pattern in the dance. In a real sense, Kloss' print is her contribution to the ceremony, her way of sharing it.

Every Kloss etching is printed by the artist herself and it is only in the last several years that she has bought a power-driven massive press built to her specifications by Charles Brand. Her earlier press, a geared Sturges, is still on call in case the power fails. "This press," Kloss relates, "is one of the original eight made [and] was acquired in 1934, having been brought to Taos by Ralph Pearson. It traveled from one rental place to another, then rested for 20 years in the studio home we built on the mesa east of town, where there was a magnificent view in all directions. In 1965 it sojourned for a few years in southern Colorado, then returned to the present studio, built seven miles north of Taos, which also has a needed vast view. I always was interested in the fact that one other of the original group of eight Sturges presses was owned by Joseph Pennell and he raved about it in his books '. . . better than any European press. . . .'"

Gene and Phillips Kloss have developed their talents and drawn nourishment from music, books, and nature. In the Taos area they have found friendship and richness of inspiration. Their marriage is visibly one of deep affection and accomplishment. Phillips Kloss has published ten volumes of poetry and musical compositions, as well.

Gene Kloss' production has never abated. Through all the many changes of faddish taste in art, she has remained true to her own standards. In 1950 she was elected an associate member of the National Academy of Design, and to full membership in 1972. Her work is represented in top collections, many of them in the East and abroad. Kloss has not followed her prints on their journeys. She has been content to stay in the West, where her career of over 50 years has its source.

Christmas Processional—Taos, *1949. Drypoint, 10 x 13½" (25 x 34 cm). First prize, Chicago Society of Etchers, 1951. Collection Edwin B. Nelson.*

Regina Tatum Cooke

Regina Tatum Cooke. Courtesy The Taos News.

REGINA TATUM COOKE arrived in Taos in 1933 with her six-year-old son, her talents for painting and writing, and plucky determination.

As a girl, Regina Tatum and her father, Judge Reese Tatum of Dalhart, Texas, had spent a vacation in Taos. (Her mother, Frances Hunter Tatum, a painter, had died when Regina was very young.) They had traveled by car over the crude roads and enjoyed the village before there were many tourist facilities. The family was art-minded and sought out the resident artists in their home-studios.

Tatum sent his daughter back to his birthplace in Tennessee where she attended Ward-Belmont, a fine finishing school for gracious young ladies. She then studied under Swedish artist Birger Sandzen at Bethany College in Lindsborg, Kansas. Sandzen painted vigorous, bright scenes of the Rocky Mountains and Rio Grande Valley. He was a friend of and exhibited with the Taos Society of Artists, and he had a strong influence on Cooke. Before graduation from Colorado College in Colorado Springs, Cooke studied art at the Broadmoor Art Academy.

Her brief marriage ended in divorce and Cooke decided to leave Denver, where her art had been exhibited at the Denver Museum, and go to Taos. She studied for two years with Walter Ufer before his death, his only pupil at the time, and is an authority on his methods, which suited her own style of realism.

During the early '40s, Cooke painted a series of oil paintings of historical missions in New Mexico as they had once been. Her reconstructions were featured in the book *Mission Monuments of New Mexico* by Edgar Hewitt and Reginald Fisher. The paintings were commissioned by the Works Progress Administration and are owned by the Museum of Fine Arts, Santa Fe.

There is a solid plastic form in Cooke's painting. She had a part in the regional period that flowered during the '30s and that recorded so much of prewar small-town America, before the influx of the short-order sameness that began to dominate and equalize the scene. Cooke's true renderings of Taos present us with a perceived kinship between adobe walls and the earth from which they were made. They are lighted with a strong, natural light and are painted with an honest, talented objectivity.

The late art historian E. Boyd wrote a comment in her review of the 1935 annual New Mexico Artist's Show at the Fine Arts Museum describing her reaction to Cooke's entry: "Grave and true, it is perfectly composed, without a false note, and grows on one indefinitely."

Over the years Cooke has been involved in numerous civic projects, such as stimulating the founding of the notable art collection owned by the Taos Public Schools (the project was continued by Alice Kinzinger, who became the art supervisor). She also assisted in the birth of the present Taos Art Association in 1952 and served as its secretary.

"Art is what put Taos on the map," she has said. She fervently encourages the reputation of Taos as an art colony and is well known and respected for her contributions to its documentation.

Cooke's later career has been spent as an award-winning journalist. Her articles about the artists of Taos form a long, engaging record stretching back to 1948 and her first job on the *Taos Star*. Newspapers came and went, but she kept writing. She worked on *El Crepusculo de la Libertad*, whose editor was the esteemed writer Frank Waters, and she continues to fill her sensitive role as recorder of the arts for the *Taos News* and also sends out a monthly column to an art magazine. Many other artists owe their fame to the discerning words Regina Tatum Cooke has penned.

ANDREW DASBURG, Tree and Valley. *Watercolor 15½ x 21½″ (39 x 55 cm). Collection Mr. and Mrs. Gerald P. Peters.*

ANDREW DASBURG, Tulips. *Oil, 16 x 20″ (41 x 51 cm).*
Collection Mrs. J.R. Modrall.

ANDREW DASBURG, Woodstock Landscape, 1910. *Oil, 8 x 10″ (20 x 25 cm).*
Courtesy Mr. and Mrs. Woodrow Wilson.

BARBARA LATHAM, Tourist Town–Taos. *Egg tempera, 24 x 35¾" (61 x 91 cm).*
Permanent Collection Roswell Museum and Art Center, Roswell, New Mexico.

CADY WELLS, Landscape: Black Mountains. *Watercolor, 13¾ x 19" (15 x 48 cm). Permanent*
Collection Roswell Museum Art Center, Roswell, New Mexico. Gift of Mr. Paul Horgan.

HELEN GREENE BLUMENSCHEIN, Piedra Lumbre. *Oil, 26 x 52" (66 x 132 cm). Collection the artist.*

ILA McAFEE, Sage Meditations. *Oil, 30 x 36" (76 x 91 cm). Private collection.*

REGINA TATUM COOKE, February Mists. *Oil, 20 x 25″ (51 x 64 cm). Collection Dr. and Mrs. Ashley Pond.*

ILA McAFEE, Buffalo Dance—Taos Pueblo, *1930s. Watercolor, 15 x 22″ (38 x 56 cm). Collection Ila McAfee.*

JOHN YOUNG-HUNTER, Signal Fire. *Oil, 48 x 48″ (122 x 122 cm). Collection John B. Wilkinson.*

LEON GASPARD, Indian Corn Dance. *Pastel, 26 x 36" (66 x 91 cm). Collection Harrison Eiteljorg.*

LEON GASPARD, Navajo Women. *Pastel, 28 x 22″ (71 x 56 cm). Fenn Galleries Ltd., Santa Fe.*

LEON GASPARD, Señor Reyna. *Oil, 10¾ x 9½" (27 x 24 cm). Collection Harrison Eiteljorg.*

LEON GASPARD, Flowers. *Oil, 12½ x 18½″ (32 x 47 cm). Collection Harrison Eiteljorg.*

NICOLAI FECHIN, Taos Indian Child. *Oil, 25 x 15" (64 x 38 cm). Fenn Galleries Ltd., Santa Fe.*

NICOLAI FECHIN, Taos Pueblo. *Oil, 25½ x 40½″ (65 x 103 cm). Collection Harrison Eiteljorg.*

NICOLAI FECHIN, Geronimo. *Oil, 18 x 14″ (46 x 36 cm). Collection Harrison Eiteljorg.*

EMIL BISTTRAM, Taos Pueblo. *Oil, 42 x 48″ (107 x 122 cm). Collection Harrison Eiteljorg.*

ROBERT HENRI, Miguel of Tesuque. *Oil on canvas, 24″ x 20″ (61 x 51 cm).*
The Anschutz Collection, Denver.

Doel Reed

DOEL REED is a tall gentleman with a supple stride who usually wears a sportcoat and a natty tweed hat in town. His brisk walks from Martha's of Taos, his daughter's chic shop, to La Doña Luz for lunch are punctuated with smiles and waves to the many friends he has made in the past 20 years.

Although he came to Taos later than most artists of the early period, he is associated with them through his long residence there, his subject matter, and the spirit of his work. From 1924 until his retirement in 1959, Reed was Chairman of the Art Department at Oklahoma State University in Stillwater. He began visiting Taos in the '40s during the gas rationing days of World War II.

The National Academy of Design recognized the excellence of Reed's aquatints by electing him to full membership in 1952. His prints are in notable museum collections throughout the United States and Europe. He does the printing himself on a small press made for him years ago by his students.

Brooding prints by Goya first attracted him to aquatint early in his career. His style is one he worked out for himself in self-demanding experimentation. Familiarity with two disciplines gives his work the stamp of authority. These are architecture, which he studied before taking his art training at the Cincinnati Art Academy (interrupted by service in World War I), and geology, which a faculty colleague took the trouble to explain.

Reed contrasts rich blacks against sparkling whites both in the solid areas and in passages of freely drawn tracery. Surprisingly, he does not capture the Taos sunlight in his dramatically staged prints. It is the foreboding sense of ancient mystery. His aquatints are of somber scenes, lit with an arbitrary light and shadowed in an impenetrable darkness, giving an effect somewhere between night and day in an unspecified timelessness.

For his subjects, Reed focuses on the Spanish culture of the valley rather than the Indian, and favors molded adobe walls—some only remnants—closed and silent Catholic chapels, and decorative graveyards. On the other hand, in his pure landscapes, Reed presents sculptured geologic formations offset by stylized vegetation under theatrical skies. His intimate knowledge of the area stems from hours wandering into the bush with crayon and ink.

The aquatint is given a soft quality by the rosin sprinkled over the metal plate before it is exposed to acid. When the resulting design is printed, a myriad of little dots of ink seem to merge, making a tone that is separate from the hatched look of a straight line etching. Reed controls the etching process of aquatint masterfully, and this is best seen in his nudes, whose classically round forms are subtly shaded in a range of values.

Reed is such an open, gregarious man, a teller of grand yarns that are never mean but always funny, that it is easy to miss the wellsprings of emotion that nourish his creative output in etching, oil, and casein. He is a passionate artist for whom Taos has been a deep, continuing inspiration.

Reed and his wife Elizabeth, a watercolorist, live in gracious comfort south of Taos, where three pink adobe buildings make up his home, his orderly studio, and the home of his daughter. Looking out his north window he has a clear view of the wide valley, the towering mountains, and the changing sky that are so much a part of his work.

Forgotten Valley, *1957. Aquatint, 10 x 17⁶ " (25 x 45 cm). Collection Metropolitan Museum of Art, New York.*

Dorothy Brett

Courtesy Fenn Galleries Ltd., Santa Fe.

THE LURE OF TAOS, aided and abetted by the magnetism of Mabel Dodge Luhan, attracted an exotic mixture of people to the village. Some, such as D. H. Lawrence, stayed only briefly, but others remained, and one of them was Lady Dorothy Brett. Usually referred to as "The Brett" by the inner circle in Taos, this long-lived and remarkable woman added a charming eccentricity to the art colony.

She was the daughter of Viscount Esher, a close advisor to Queen Victoria. She and her sister took their dancing classes at Windsor Castle. The sister went on to become the Ranee of Sarawak and remained true to her class, but Dorothy became a Bohemian in the original sense of the word.

She chopped off her hair and entered the Slade Art School, where she studied under Augustus John, and took up with the renowned Bloomsbury Group. Her closest friend then was Katherine Mansfield; others were George Bernard Shaw, Leopold Stokowski, Virginia Woolf, Aldous and John Huxley, Bertrand Russell, and, of course, D. H. and Frieda Lawrence. There are many Brett sketches of these people done in sinuous pencil line à la Augustus John and Art Nouveau from the period.

At 27, Brett was already deaf. Until late in her life she carried an ear-trumpet and complained of its awkwardness, but she never let it get her down. A battery-operated hearing aid made her old age more comfortable and gave her the advantage of turning it off at will. Throughout her life she had a beguilingly alert, youthful humor. Her face was pert. In youth she was small and pretty with an alluringly ample figure. She dressed in exotic smocks, Indian gear, and bejeweled headbands.

When the Lawrences were invited to Taos by Mabel Dodge, Brett came, too. She was 30 in 1924 and she adored Lawrence, but she did not give up Taos to follow him.

Her adobe house, a modest place with a spacious studio and bed-sitting extension, stuck out like a forlorn cottage where two major roads meet north of town. Yet on its door, with wry humor, she painted her family crest. To get inside, often as not, you climbed over a makeshift chicken-wire screen meant to hold in her dachshund.

Well into her late years, Brett painted. Her work can seem almost childlike—lacking in perspective, riotous with color, aswirl in decorative line. But beneath this surface naiveté, Brett had an uncanny way of sensing the basic rhythms of her favorite subject, the Taos Indian celebrations. To portray them dancing, Brett recreated patterns of movement as organizations of pictorial elements. It was done almost instinctively. Her six years at the Slade gave her an approach to style, but her art was of herself.

Her abundant work includes portraits, single Indian dancers, landscapes, and mystic or symbolic paintings. Some of them are memorable images, very much connected to her own emotions and to those of the Indians whom she admired.

Brett died in Taos in August 1977, where she had lived for 93 years, lonely for those she had outlived, tired in body, but sparkling with ready friendship and appreciation for visitors. For one who had had so much, it is a wonder that she spent years of her life content to go fishing, visit the pueblo, and paint, paint, paint. There is no one like her and she will always be missed. Her storybook life has been the subject of several books; one of the best is her own *Lawrence and Brett.*

The First Born, *1937. Oil, 59 x 24" (150 x 61 cm).*
Collection Museum of Fine Arts,
Museum of New Mexico, Santa Fe.
Gift of The Millicent Rogers Foundation.

Hopi Snake Dance. *Oil, 24 x 37" (61 x 94 cm). McAdoo Galleries, Inc., Woodrow Wilson Fine Arts, Santa Fe.*

John Young-Hunter

Courtesy Fenn Galleries Ltd., Santa Fe.

JOHN YOUNG-HUNTER was born in Glasgow, Scotland, in 1874. His father, Colin Hunter, was a well-known marine artist and a close friend of John Singer Sargent, under whom John Young-Hunter studied at the Royal Academy. His background was that of a highborn member of British society and his handsome, aquiline good looks were appropriate to his class.

Young-Hunter met with early success in England. His work hung at the Tate Gallery and in Paris at the Musée de Luxembourg. He then spent five years in New York where he became a successful portrait painter of fashionable people.

As a boy in England, like Dorothy Brett, he saw the Buffalo Bill Wild West Show when it played for Queen Victoria. That planted a seed of curiosity which later brought him to Taos. In 1917, armed with a letter of introduction to Bert Phillips, he became an immediate member of the inner circle and a friend of Mabel Dodge, who was then married to Maurice Sterne. He later became close to Tony Luhan, Mabel Dodge's third and last husband.

In his posthumously published book, *Reviewing the Years*, Young-Hunter said of Mabel Dodge Luhan: ". . .her contributions to our community are not mythical—for she enriched immeasurably the artistic and cultural life, not only of our Town but our Time."

Eventually, Young-Hunter built his own studio in Taos and lived on as a productive artist until his death in 1955.

Among his patrons was the Wilkinson family who had met the artist on their trips to Taos. Mrs. Wilkinson admired his painting *The Camp Fire* and, with reluctance, Young-Hunter sold it to Mr. Wilkinson as an anniversary gift. Young-Hunter later wrote to them in his courtly fashion:

"Your picture was painted shortly after my arrival in Taos. Having come here almost directly from the East by way of Montana, I was moved to enthusiastic appreciation of the beauty of this land and its history. The Indians belong to the Pueblo adjoining this town (of Taos) and the background is my interpretation of the impressive Sangre de Cristo mountains which surround us. It was the Life of the people here, particularly the Indian that aroused my imagination .... The Charming simplicity of the Indian Life intrigued me .... often had I seen them sitting around a small camp-fire, sometimes singing, sometimes just sitting contemplatively exchanging thoughts without the necessity for constant chatter."

Young-Hunter's work has a wet bravura quality and his colors are tastefully planned. In passages of brushwork, there is often a boldness like that of his mentor, John Singer Sargent. He did strong watercolors of Taos landscapes and many paintings on an Indian theme, but he was more widely known for his portraits. He sometimes combined egg tempera with oil. His handsome portrait of Mabel Dodge Luhan belongs to the Harwood Foundation, which held a memorial exhibition for him in 1956.

Leon Gaspard

Leon Gaspard in his studio. Courtesy The Gaspard Museum, Taos.

LEON GASPARD was a thoroughly romantic figure whose life reads better than most fiction. He was advised to go West by Caruso's doctor in order to recover from injuries incurred when he jumped out of a French observation plane just before it crashed in World War I. Because Gaspard was married to the daughter of a wealthy American widow, he had been brought to the United States from the hospital in France.

The Gaspards arrived in Santa Fe and were met by Sheldon Parsons, the affable host to all visiting artists, who advised them to go to Taos. They stayed a few months on that first visit in 1915 and returned again in 1918.

Gaspard was born in 1882 in Vitebsk, Russia, where he was a boyhood classmate of Marc Chagall. He studied art in Odessa and Paris; here he developed his reputation and personal style. Although impressionistic in his touch, Gaspard created an amalgam of Russian embroidery and vibrant color with a freedom from all cant. His early inspirations were the sights and people of Mongolia and Tibet. He saw parallels to the Oriental people in the Pueblo Indians of Taos.

After settling in Taos, Gaspard returned to Russia and traveled through Asia, Mongolia, Tibet and China on a long adventurous trip with his wife. They returned to Taos in 1921 and built a fabled home, which is now open to the public, in a mixture of the exotic elements of Russian architecture and the traditions of adobe architecture.

It was some time before the successful, alien Gaspard found acceptance in Taos. He was a bit eccentric and arrogant, but eventually he became friends with the early group, especially with Buck Dunton who studied with him and, in exchange, took him to the best fishing holes.

After his wife Evelyn died in 1956, Gaspard at 74 was bereft, but he made a happy marriage with Dora Kaminsky, an artist and long-time friend of the Gaspards. Their marriage brought a late bloom to his life. A world tour through Europe to Russia inspired him to paint again and he enjoyed a success he had not had for a long time.

Gaspard's paintings have a strong individual style. The portraits, scenes, and costumes he painted were outlined with sketchy lines that enclosed jeweled insets of color. These bright colors were often surrounded by quantities of white or pastel neutrals.

Gaspard died in Taos in 1964. A fine tribute to him, a book entitled *Leon Gaspard*, was written that year by Frank Waters. Today, paintings by Gaspard are in great demand and command prices as high as $100,000.

Nicolai Fechin

Nicolai Fechin in his studio. Courtesy Fenn Galleries Ltd., Santa Fe.

ANOTHER TRANSPLANT from Russia was Nicolai Fechin, who was born in Kazan on November 26, 1881. As a boy he was sickly and shy. He helped his father carve and paint icons at which he showed exceptional ability. After a delayed graduation from elementary school, he entered the new Kazan Art School where he did very well in his studies.

Fechin's father lost his business and deserted his family. His mother, too, left him and returned to her own family. With the help of an aunt and uncle, he tried the entry examinations of the Imperial Academy of Art in St. Petersburg. Though he was financially destitute, his work so impressed the staff that they allowed him to enter.

His student career was studded with successes; in his final year in 1909, he was given his degree and a prize of 2000 rubles for his painting *Gathering of the Cabbage Crop*. Before graduation he had already joined his alma mater as a teacher in Kazan.

The colorful life and costumes of the varied ethnic groups near Kazan furnished Fechin with his early subjects. In 1910 he sent two portraits to the Carnegie Institute in Pittsburgh for an exhibition. His work began to reap praise and interest in the United States. One of his admirers was W.S. Stimmel of Pittsburgh, who began a correspondence with Fechin. Needing help on his translations of these letters, Fechin turned to the beautiful, aristocratic daughter of the art school director, Alexandra Belkovich, who was then just a child. Fechin married her in 1913 when she was only a teenager.

World War I sealed Fechin off from his western patrons and the American competitive shows he had been entering. With Stimmel's help, he, Alexandra, and their daughter Eya emigratèd to New York and he entered the art world of the city. Alexandra acted as his interpreter. He found a ready market for his portraits and saved money for his trip to Taos by train in 1927.

The portrait painter John Young-Hunter was Fechin's host in Taos. Once Fechin saw the village with the wooded landscape and mountainous backdrop and the population of Asiatic-looking people wearing colorful costumes, he arranged to stay. He bought land and built a home and studio in a mixture of Spanish, Pueblo, and Russian style. He built much of it himself, and carved both the beams and the furniture.

Taos and Fechin were a dynamic combination. There he produced a flood of paintings. They were mostly portraits, but he also painted landscapes and still lifes—and produced drawings and sculpture.

A Fechin painting is unique and uncopiable, although many artists have copied its surface effects. On a porous white ground, considered by scholars to be chemically unstable, Fechin applied his paint alla prima, often with a knife. The ground absorbed the oil from the pigment, leaving mounds and strokes of unmixed color on the surface with a distinctive brilliance that does not rely on gloss, only on the prismatic effect of the color itself.

Fechin described his models with telling strokes, but the figure melds into a background that is usually an abstraction of freely applied strokes. Faces and hands might be smooth and more detailed than the costume.

Fechin was a student of Ilya Repin, one of the towering figures of pre-communist Russian Impressionism. In Russia impressionism was a gutsy, strong style with a vibrant, not a pastel, palette. Fechin brought this style to America and developed the appreciation for it here. Of late, an interest in Fechin has been felt in Russia and exchange exhibitions have been arranged; paintings executed in Russia have toured the United States while those created here were touring Russia. Among those shown at an impressive exhibition at the Fenn Galleries of Santa Fe was a penetrating large painting of Lenin. It had the gripping magnetism in the eyes that characterizes Fechin's portraits and made an unforgettable impression of a man destined for history. At the time it was painted, Lenin had yet to fill the role that was later to be his.

After an unhappy turn late in his marriage, Fechin left Taos and established an art school in Santa Monica, California, where he remained until his death in 1955.

Geronimo. *Charcoal, 18 x 14" (46 x 36 cm). Collection Harrison Eiteljorg.*

Emil Bisttram

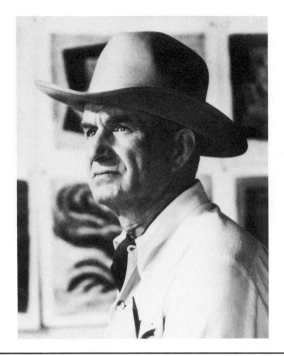

WHEN EMIL BISTTRAM arrived in Taos in 1932 and established his Taos School of Art, he brought with him a devotion to the principles of Dynamic Symmetry. He had studied this classic method of composition under Howard Giles at the New York School of Fine and Applied Art and then had taught it at the Roerich Museum in the Master Institute of Art, also in New York. On a Guggenheim Fellowship in 1931 he studied fresco painting with Diego Rivera in Mexico.

Bisttram made an immediate impact on Taos. He was always a civic-minded man who interacted with business leaders just as well as he did with the art community. It was his habit to meet men from the town for coffee sometimes twice a day, and he often tried to enlist their support for the cause of art. He was instrumental in founding the Heptagon Gallery, which included seven artists of a contemporary persuasion. (The group later expanded, moved its gallery a few times, and then floundered.) In 1952 Bisttram was one of the instigators of the Taos Art Association. This enterprising group, who created the Stables Gallery in 1953 for their members, still flourishes. Bisttram served as its president three times and was in office when he died in 1976.

Despite his civic, business, and art activities, it was through his paintings that Bisttram most deeply affected the art colony, for his was a contemporary, experimental style, always changing. Using similar subject matter, he created work conceptually different from that of the original artists of Taos.

Bisttram was born in Hungary in 1895 and arrived in the United States at the age of seven. His speech was without noticeable accent. He was a well-proportioned, slender man who always wore a neat Stetson, sports jacket, and trim clothes. His opinions were sought as a writer, speaker, teacher, and juror. Though young, Bisttram was already an artist of stature when he arrived in Taos. His watercolors had earned honors in New York and his frescoes for the Taos Court House showed Rivera's influence in their strong simple forms and social message.

There was no single Bisttram style, because he attempted to make each painting a completely new state-

ment; but several characteristics of his work seem to be present in most of his paintings: He relied on bright, flat color and clear contours. There is a sophisticated folk quality about some of his paintings, and a touch of surrealism. His work could become almost totally abstract, while still retaining the same contour and color sense of his more pictorial work.

In a lecture early in the summer of 1957, "On Understanding Contemporary Art," Emil Bisttram opened with an historical survey that is among the most condensed and well-worded theories available on his theme. His thesis is that a nation is an entity that expresses its spirit in various forms, including art. In particular, a nation expresses its beliefs about those unseen aspects of life that are the concern of its religion and philosophy. After the survey of Chinese, Egyptian, and Renaissance expression in art, Bisttram addressed the present United States. Among his ideas were these:

"We are in the midst of a struggle to reach maturity, contending with many factors. . . . Our dynamic energy, symbolic of youth, expresses itself through mass production, the manufacturing of an infinite number of items, the development of trade. This does not leave room for creative thought and contemplation of life.

"We all recognize that this is a scientific age. Science searches into the mysteries of life and the forces that animate it. . . . I feel that the creative effort in the field of art today is closely related to psychology and science.

" . . . the new era in art, a new age, a new renaissance, is attempting to express the spirit, the essence of things, that which is felt. . . . These works demand that we contemplate them in silence, receptive to whatever stimuli may be in the work, allowing our own intuitions and creative imaginations to participate and, in the process become 'at one' with the creative form. In other words, we who look . . . become creators, too."

Clearly, the arrival of Bisttram and his intellectual viewpoint marked a change in the Taos art colony that began in 1898. He is one of the signals that the old legend was ending and a new one was in the process of becoming.

Hopi Snake Dance. *Oil, 41 x 45" (104 x 114 cm). Collection Museum of Fine Arts, Museum of New Mexico, Santa Fe.*

THE VISITORS
Robert Henri, John Marin, Marsden Hartley

AOS LURED MANY luminaries from the eastern art establishment. They came, they painted, and they went away. There was an interaction between the visitors and the stayers; and derivative remnants of imported styles spread with a ripple effect briefly and then were absorbed.

Among those who came, you might question which was the greater impulse—to leave behind the stamp of their personalities or to take away the lasting memories of a place inhabited by two closed societies, the Indian and the Spanish. Surely in the lives of Robert Henri, John Marin, and Marsden Hartley, New Mexico filled a special place.

ROBERT HENRI
Robert Henri was an articulate, Messianic man exhilarated by the power of his thoughts. He inspired his students, among them Andrew Dasburg, with a zealous sense of their mission to create. Besides his well-developed philosophy, he had a well-practiced technique. Wherever he went, his subject was people. There is a Henri look: the wet lip with a brilliant highlight on its full, sculptured form, the shiny black hair, the florid skin—all executed in the creamy, blunt strokes with which he built the faces of his models.

Henri was invited to New Mexico to paint the Indians by an esteemed scholar Dr. Edgar L. Hewett, director of the School of American Research in Santa Fe. He visited Taos and a number of pueblos in New Mexico from a base in Santa Fe in 1916, 1918, and again in 1922. There are fine examples of his work in New Mexico collections. It was Henri's desire to paint strong, classic portraits in the manner of Frans Hals, and he succeeded.

Pat Trenton, Curator of American Art at the Denver Art Museum, quoted Henri from an interview published in 1916 by the *Santa Fe New Mexican* in her *Picturesque Images From Taos and Santa Fe:* "There is something beautiful... strong, noble in every living thing. It is our business to find it and in the search of it we find our own happiness."

Such a philosophy is close in spirit to that of the original artists of Taos. When Henri died in 1929, he was one of the most influential minds in American art.

JOHN MARIN
John Marin was an eccentric man who found his niche as a painter at about the age of 40, after which he was supported by the unfailing enthusiasm of Alfred Stieglitz. In the overlapping salon of Mabel Dodge and the Stieglitz circle, the gentle, humorous, gifted Marin had a welcome membership. He was a guest of Mabel Dodge Luhan at her Taos compound in 1929 and again in 1930.

Marin had invented a landscape style of brief, abstract notations in diluted and well-mixed colors that is markedly his own—and yet, in Taos his manner of encoding landscape into brushstrokes met and jibed almost perfectly with that developed by resident artist Victor Higgins. Marin loved to fish and he enjoyed the easy comradeship of the other artists on fishing-painting expeditions into Hondo Canyon and elsewhere. Higgins was his companion on some of these outings. The men saw things alike in that they perceived the thrusts and quietnesses of the vast landscape, and recorded them with brevity. Marin both gave and took from the ambience of the New Mexico scene. His paintings are not really separate from his scenes of Maine except in subject matter. In Taos he had to create new schema to account for the boldness of soaring mountains and flat clouds that tend to hover as echoes over horizontal mesas. His renderings of these sights were somewhat less abstract than

his eastern landscapes in some cases. They seem to have a solid virility and power. This strength might be the most important effect his trips to the Southwest had on his work.

Marin was a watercolorist. His paintings were serious and complete work, not just sketches for future oils. His dedication to watercolor and his freely inventive control of it did not go unnoticed in Taos, especially in the group around Dasburg who responded to Marin's fusion of cubistic fragmentation with his own idiosyncratic style.

MARSDEN HARTLEY

Marsden Hartley, though born in Maine, was in Germany at the beginning of World War I and was greatly affected by German expressionism. He was in the forefront of the modern movement, despite his labored style. Henry Geldzahler made a most astute and unusual comment about Hartley in his book *American Painting in the 20th Century:* "Marsden Hartley produced an art that is a triumph of the need for expression over a lack of facility. There is nothing gracious or easy about his talent, and his finest work, dramatic rather than lyric, seems always blunt and stunted."

Hartley exhibited in the Armory Show of 1913 and the Forum Exhibition of 1916. He was one of the Stieglitz circle. In 1919 he made a trip to New Mexico. His response to the brooding mountains and to the artifacts of Spanish Catholicism was to give vent to dark feelings of gloom in his emotional work. Hartley used pigment as a dense, malleable material. His forms were boldly conceived, sometimes ugly in contour.

For the summer months and part of the fall, Hartley remained in Taos, and then wintered into 1920 in Santa Fe.

He viewed the work of other artists who had visited the Southwest as weak in concept and lacking in an intellectual grasp of what was possible in art. His own solid juxtapositions of forms, often roughly textured, and his clearly defined boundary lines appealed to such open-minded artists as Blumenschein. Yet, Blumenschein created richer patterns with more empathy for the locale. It is unwise to draw conclusions of influences, but there have been traces of Hartley's painting style in the work of several painters, including B. J. O. Nordfelt, who is more associated with Santa Fe than Taos.

In Hartley's life, New Mexico was a presence to be worked out in recollections painted some time later. He was still painting New Mexican themes even while living in Berlin in 1922 and 1923. Hartley traveled widely as he searched out the typical vistas and forms associated with the exotic, and Taos was an exotic place to him. Only late in his life, when he went back to Maine, did he find his special place. He died in Maine in 1943.

There were numbers of artists-visitors who refreshed the artists of Taos with their new views and styles, but these three men serve to make the point that Taos affected artists enough for them to make the trip to see it, to experience it, and to try to express it.

Their images carried the message that Taos was an important art colony within a distinctive environment—a small place in a grandiose setting which, once seen, was never forgotten. Creative people—writers, musicians, actors as well as artists—still continue to find an impulse there toward probing their own talents. Taos still beckons.

Bibliography

BOOKS

Balcom, Mary. *Nicholai Fechin.* Flagstaff, Arizona: Northland Press, 1975.

Bickerstaff, Laura. *Pioneer Artists of Taos.* Denver: Sage Books, 1955.

Blumenschein, Helen Greene. *Recuerdos/Early Days of the Blumenschein Family.* Silver City, New Mexico: Tecolete Press, 1979. (Available from the Kit Carson Foundation, Taos.)

Border, Patricia Janis. *Paintings of the American West.* New York: Abrams, 1979.

Coke, Van Deren. *Andrew Dasburg.* Albuquerque: University of New Mexico Press, 1979.

—. *Taos and Santa Fe/ The Artist's Environment/ 1882-1942.* Albuquerque: University of New Mexico Press, 1963.

Dawdy, Doris Ostrander. *Artists of the American West.* Chicago: Swallow Press, 1974.

Geldzahler, Henry. *American Painting in the 20th Century.* New York: Metropolitan Museum of Art, 1965.

Henri, Robert. *The Art Spirit.* Philadelphia: Lippincott, 1923.

Luhan, Mabel Dodge. *Taos and Its Artists.* New York: Duel, Sloan, and Pierce, 1979.

McCracken, Harold. *Nicholai Fechin.* New York: Hammer Galleries, 1961.

Morrill, Claire. *A Taos Mosaic/ Portrait of a New Mexico Village.* Albuquerque: University of New Mexico Press, 1973.

New Mexico Artists. Special edition of *New Mexico Quarterly.* Albuquerque: University of New Mexico Press, 1952.

Reich, Sheldon. *John Marin.* Tucson: University of Arizona Press, 1970.

Waters, Frank. *Leon Gaspard.* Flagstaff, Arizona: Northland Press, 1964.

Young-Hunter, John. *Reviewing the Years.* New York: Crown, 1963.

CATALOGS

Branham, Eya Fechin and Fenn, Forrest. *Nicholai Fechin.* Santa Fe: Fenn Galleries, 1975.

Bywaters, Jerry. *Andrew Dasburg.* New York: American Federation of the Arts, 1959.

Chase, Katherin. *The Blumenscheins of Taos.* Flagstaff: Museum of Northern Arizona, 1979.

Coke, Van Deren. *Kenneth M. Adams/A Retrospective Exhibition.* Albuquerque: Museum of Art, University of New Mexico, 1964.

—. *Marin in New Mexico, 1929-1930.* Albuquerque: Museum of Art, University of New Mexico, 1968.

Dick, Ruth W., ed. *Kenneth M. Adams, N.A.* Albuquerque: Western Art Gallery, 1972.

Durham, Linda and Monacelli, Linda. *Santa Fe Salutes.* Santa Fe: Santa Fe Festival of the Arts, 1977.

Ewing, Robert E. *Victor Higgins.* Santa Fe: Museum of New Mexico, 1972.

Fenn, Forrest. *Nicholai Fechin/ An Exhibition on Loan from the Soviet Socialist Republics.* Santa Fe: Fenn Galleries, 1975.

— and McCracken, Harold. *E. Irving Couse.* Santa Fe; Fenn Galleries, 1974.

Hennings, William T. *Ernest L. Blumenschein Retrospective.* Colorado Springs: Colorado Springs Fine Arts Center, 1968.

Hewitt, Edgar L. and Schriever, George. *Representative Art and Artists of New Mexico.* Santa Fe: School of American Research, Museum of New Mexico, 1940. Reprint, Olan Gallery, 1976.

Porter, Dean. *Victor Higgins.* Notre Dame, Indiana: University of Notre Dame, 1975.

Schriever, George. *American Masters in the West.* Oklahoma City: National Cowboy Hall of Fame, 1974.

ARTICLES

Adams, Kenneth M. "Los Ocho Pintores." *New Mexico Quarterly*, Summer 1951, pp. 146-152.

"Appreciation of Indian Art." *El Palacio*, May 1919, p. 178. (Interview with E.L. Blumenschein and Bert G. Phillips.)

"Artists of Santa Fe." *American Heritage*, February 1976, pp. 57-72.

Bisttram, Emil. "On Understanding Contemporary Art." *El Palacio*, July 1957, pp. 201-208. Also in *The New Mexico Quarterly*, August 1957.

Blair, Billie. "Chronicler of the Arts, Regina Tatum Cooke." *The Taos News*, 15 September 1977, pp. 52-53.

Booth, Mary Witter. "The Taos Art Colony." *El Palacio*, November 1946, pp. 318-323.

Blumenschein, Ernest L. "Artists of Taos, Howard Cook." *El Palacio*, March 1946, pp. 53-55.

Briesen, Asha. "Andrew Dasburg." *The Taos News*, 28 April 1977.

Cassidy, Ina Sizer. "Art and Artists of New Mexico." A series of articles published in *New Mexico Magazine* on:

Oscar Berninghaus, January 1933, p. 28.
Emil Bisttram, September 1934, p. 17.
Ernest L. Blumenschein, July 1932, p. 31.
Eanger Irving Couse, August 1932, p. 31.
W. Herbert Dunton, December 1932, p. 22.
Victor Higgins, December 1932, p. 22.
John Ward Lockwood, February 1933, p. 27.
Bert Geer Phillips, July 1932, p. 31.
Joseph Henry Sharp, August 1932, p. 31.
Walter Ufer, January 1933, p. 28.

Cooke, Regina Tatum, ed. "70 Years of Taos Art." *The Taos News*, 12 September 1968.

Davis, Laura A. "An Indian Painter of the West." *El Palacio*, 1 September 1922, pp. 65-69.

Fisher, Reginald. "E. Martin Hennings, Artist of Taos." *El Palacio*, August 1946.

Harvey, Betty. "E. Irving Couse." *Artists of the Rockies*, Winter 1977, pp. 28-37.

Nelson, Mary Carroll. "Andrew Dasburg: Taos Maverick." *American Artist*, April 1979, p. 64.

—. "Gene Kloss: Intaglio Artist." *American Artist*, February 1978, p. 64.

—. "Doel Reed: Aquatints from the Heartland." *American Artist*, May 1979, p. 66.

—, with Egri, Kit and Ted. "The Pioneer Artists of Taos." Special issue of *American Artist*, January 1978.

Phillips, Bert G. Caption for catalog. *El Palacio*, July 1920, p. 235.

Ufer, Walter. "The Santa Fe-Taos Colony." *El Palacio*, August 1916, pp. 75-81.

Waters, Frank. "Nicholai Fechin." *Arizona Highways*, February 1952, pp. 14-27.

Watson, E.W. "Howard Cook." *American Artist*, March 1945, pp. 8-13. (Interview.)

White, Robert Rankin. "The Life of E. Martin Hennings, 1886-1956." *El Palacio*, Fall 1978, pp. 21-36.

UNPUBLISHED MANUSCRIPTS

Black, Dorothy Skousen. "A Study of Taos as an Art Colony and of Representative Taos Painters." Unpublished master's thesis. Albuquerque: University of New Mexico, 1959.

Kline, Vivian. "Joseph Henry Sharp: Indian Painter and Conformist." Cincinnati: Cincinnati Art Museum, 1972.

INTERVIEWS

Dorothy Brett, Dorothy Berninghaus Brandenburg, Helen Greene Blumenschein, Howard Cook, Regina Tatum Cooke, Kibbey Couse, Alfred Dasburg, Andrew Dasburg, Helen Hennings, Gene Kloss, Barbara Latham, Sarah Higgins Mack, Ila McAfee, Doel Reed, and the townspeople of Taos.

PRIVATE PAPERS

The Blumenschein Letters. State Archives, Santa Fe.

The Catherine Carter Critcher File. Corcoran Gallery, Washington, D.C. Courtesy Calista Hillman.

The Dasburg Letters. Courtesy Alfred Dasburg.

The Phillips Memorabilia. Courtesy Bill Beutler and Forrest Fenn.

The Phillips Family Photographs. Courtesy Jack Boyer, Kit Carson Foundation, Taos.

Index

Edited by Bonnie Silverstein
Designed by Bob Fillie
Graphic production by Ellen Greene
Set in 9-point century expanded